SUMMERTIME

Galton Blackiston's
SUMMERTIME

Photography by Tara Fisher

Virgin BOOKS

Published by Virgin Books 2009

2 4 6 8 10 9 7 5 3 1

Copyright © Galton Blackiston 2009
Photography © Tara Fisher 2009

Galton Blackiston has asserted his right under the Copyright, Designs
and Patents Act 1988 to be identified as the author of this work

First published in Great Britain in 2009 by
Virgin Books
Random House, 20 Vauxhall Bridge Road,
London SW1V 2SA

www.virginbooks.com
www.rbooks.co.uk

Addresses for companies within The Random House Group Limited can be found at:
www.randomhouse.co.uk/offices.htm

The Random House Group Limited Reg. No. 954009

A CIP catalogue record for this book
is available from the British Library

ISBN 9781905264636

The Random House Group Limited supports The Forest Stewardship Council [FSC], the
leading international forest certification organisation. All our titles that are printed on
Greenpeace approved FSC certified paper carry the FSC logo.
Our paper procurement policy can be found at www.rbooks.co.uk/environment

Printed and bound in Germany

CONTENTS

FOREWORD by Matthew Fort

Galton is a true food hero. He turned his back on a glittering career as a cricketer for a glittering career as a chef and as a missionary for all that is best about Norfolk and its produce.

I first came across his cooking when he represented his region in the *Great British Menu*. Galton's dishes were the kind that made me sit up and hum with pleasure. He had a brilliant cooking technique and an unerring sense of taste. It turned out that he was as engaging a fellow in the flesh as he was good a chef in the kitchen. Since then, of course, he has gone on to endear himself to countless numbers of television viewers on further series of the *Great British Menu* and on *Market Kitchen*. But he's never allowed celebrity to cloud his vision of what good cooking should be.

It's not just that he cooks food good enough to win a Michelin star. It's not just that he has fine judgement on how and why ingredients go together. He is also a passionate and eloquent advocate of Norfolk produce and Norfolk cooking. He has turned Morston Hall into a place of pilgrimage for anyone truly interested in the best of British cooking using the finest local ingredients.

But he's more than just a Michelin-starred master of the range. As his appearances on *Market Kitchen* showed, he is able to come up with dishes that are as delightful for the domestic cook to rustle up as they are delicious to eat. And here, at last, is Galton's *Summertime* cookbook, true to Galton's own approach to summer eating and true to Norfolk and its wonderful produce.

INTRODUCTION

The idea of writing a book on summertime cooking had been swimming around my head for a couple of years. I don't know whether it's just me – or perhaps it's an age thing – but I've noticed that for the past few years, come January I invariably start dreaming of the summer. Although there are certain aspects of the winter I do like – mainly Christmas with the family, with hopefully a little sprinkling of snow – it's the warmer months I really look forward to. Once the football season is out of the way, ideally with the least amount of damage possible, it's time once again to get the boat into the water and to clean up the barbecue.

My earliest memories of cooking are from childhood summer holidays on the north Norfolk coast, when we stayed at the Watch House near Blakeney. I'm the youngest of five boys and, along with my brother Jamie, I'd mess about in the water channels, cockling, shrimping and catching flat fish like dabs, butts and even the odd plaice. We'd smother the cockles with vinegar then have to keep them in our cheeks for about five minutes while the taste of the vinegar subsided! I remember making my first prawn cocktail too, which was then the height of sophistication.

We'd also watch the terns diving for whitebait, which meant they were being chased by mackerel, which we'd then try to catch ourselves. One trick was to put silver milk bottle tops in the water – the mackerel would be fooled into thinking the glint was more whitebait, and then we'd grab them!

Once we'd caught them we'd go back to the Watch House and fillet and then pan-fry them, obliged to use such simple cooking methods by the lack of facilities. We also used to dig for lugworms in the sand, then set up a line between two pieces of wood, adding baited hooks a yard apart. When the tide went out we'd leave the line and go back next morning to check on our haul.

Another source of fun was taking the boat and exploring the coastline, stopping off at Stiffkey to pick winkles and whelks on the mud flats. Of course, you had to watch out for the tides or you could get stranded! We used to pick raw samphire and eat it, but it wasn't a huge hit as it was so salty. Sea kale too. Everything we ate had to be child-friendly, although the one thing that definitely wasn't was my father's homemade wine, made from elderberries and other hedgerow produce.

Nowadays, fishing plays a large party in our family summer holidays – anything to do with the boat is highly popular with our sons, Harry and Sam, who are both real outdoorsy children. We also occasionally go fruit-picking at Wiveton Hall, just down the road near Blakeney, but the children generally just end up lobbing fruit at each other!

The summertime meals I enjoy most are the ones that take the least time to make, and this probably means salads or simply fried or grilled dishes. Or I love packing a few bits and pieces together and getting out on the marshes with my wife, Tracy, and the boys and having a picnic. My favourite thing to do is to take one of those little camping stoves and a frying pan, then go cockling, collect some samphire and catch a few brown shrimps from the creeks using a net, then use the ingredients to knock up a stir-fry; it's just brilliant fun and something I've done since I was knee-high to a grasshopper.

Summertime represents something completely different for me and, I must say, I've found it very exciting writing about dishes that will make you smile when you eat them and which are essentially uncomplicated, in most cases can be made in advance and most importantly are perfect for home cooking.

There's no doubt about it: to cook well you need good ingredients, a little confidence and really, wherever possible, to source your ingredients seasonally and, in my case, regionally. That's not to say you need to buy the most expensive ingredients around; on the contrary, good ingredients could include decent tomatoes, lovely herbs and pulses just as happily as pricey prime cuts of meat.

Although I am a professional chef, I like to think of myself as a person who loves to cook and gets excited about being able to cook simply yet well. Too many young, aspiring chefs seem to want to prove their culinary worthiness by creating unnecessarily complicated dishes, rather than letting the main ingredient speak for itself. While I'm all for trying out new combinations of ingredients, I will never risk overpowering dishes with overbearing flavours.

We have such a great larder out there, embracing so many different cultures and styles, and all it takes to make the most of it is a little knowledge and confidence – and that's what I hope this book will give you. I hope you'll follow the recipes and use them again and again, and feel free to adapt and change whenever you see fit. I would love everyone who buys this book to get it dirty – in my view there's no greater acknowledgement of a favourite book than one that has lost its cover, is completely messed up with stains and the like, as it shows how much use you've got out of it.

But above all, I hope you'll enjoy the uncomplicatedness of cooking in the summer.

BREA

KFAST

Early morning on the north Norfolk coast has an almost ethereal nature until the mist clears and the sun breaks through to burn the dew off the salt marsh reeds, blowing away the cobwebs that hang like diamond necklaces between the stalks. Curlews, gulls and terns rise from the mud flats, boats chug out for the morning catch and joggers and dog walkers amble at various paces along the coastal path. For those who are up early, breakfast punctuates the morning with the desire for hearty foods – and even people who are on holiday enjoy nothing more than the treat of a traditional English breakfast.

On a working day I start breakfast on the run with a cup of tea and a piece of toast. We are early birds at home – Sam, our youngest boy, who's eight, is always up between six and seven o'clock; this means the dog, Daisy, gets disturbed and the TV goes on and we all end up getting up very early. Like most people who lead hectic lives – I'm at Morston in the mornings and Tracy is getting the boys off to school – we don't tend to have big breakfasts during the week: the boys will eat cereals or pastries.

At weekends, Tracy does a fry-up or makes pancakes. She cooks a mean breakfast of sausages, bacon, fried bread – it's essential that it's fatty! – mushrooms, tomatoes, eggs and black pudding. Pork is generally good in Norfolk. In fact, Norfolk bacon, sausages, black pudding, gammon and pork are among the best in the country.

STRAWBERRIES £ 2.
RASPBERRIES £ 2
GOOSEBERRIES £ 1
CURRANTS £ 1.
POTATOES £ 2.
BR. BEANS £ 1
BEETROOTS £ 1
CARROTS £ 1
JAM £ 1
HONEY £ 3
EGGS £ 2.
ARTICHOKES 40p

Muesli with Poached Summer Fruits

A guest at Morston once asked me what we put in our muesli. Her view was that it should include seeds, fruits and nuts, so we started experimenting. This is my favourite combination of ingredients – the quantity of each is up to you, but it's easiest to make up a big batch and store it in an airtight container in a dry place. I love poached summer fruits and often have them myself for breakfast with yoghurt, but the addition of muesli makes for a more substantial meal. The soft fruit we use in the restaurant comes from just down the road at Blakeney, so it's full of summery freshness and juicy flavour.

1. To make the stock (sugar) syrup for poaching the fruit, place the sugar in a measuring jug then tip into the pan, then measure out the equivalent volume of water. Put the water into the pan with the sugar and allow the sugar to dissolve over a low heat, stirring once or twice, then bring to the boil and simmer gently for 4 minutes. Allow to cool and add the lemon juice.

2. Place the summer fruits in a pan, adding enough cooled syrup to just cover. Place over a medium heat and bring to a very slow simmer, poaching it just long enough for the fruit to start to soften. Remove from the heat and allow the fruit to cool in the saucepan.

3. Serve the muesli topped with poached fruit and, for a less healthy option, pour over some thick cream! The poached fruits will keep for five days in an airtight container in the fridge.

A MIXTURE OF ANY OF THE FOLLOWING:

toasted cereals (wheat, barley and oat flakes)
raisins
sultanas
dates
dried apricots
blueberries
dried mango
dried banana
sunflower seeds
pumpkin seeds
toasted coconut
roasted hazelnuts
brazil nuts

For the poached summer fruits
50g (2oz) sugar
juice of 1/2 lemon, strained
250g (9oz) strawberries, hulled
125g (41/2oz) fresh blueberries
250g (9oz) fresh raspberries
cream, to serve (optional)

Smoked Salmon with Herby Scrambled Eggs

SERVES 6

18 slices smoked salmon about 1cm (1/2 inch) thick

9 free-range eggs

grating of fresh nutmeg

50g (2oz) salted butter, cut into small pieces

1 tbsp snipped fresh chives

1 tbsp chopped fresh parsley

1 tbsp chopped fresh tarragon

1 tsp chopped fresh mint

seasoning

toasted and buttered spelt flour bread, to serve (see page 25)

The classic combination of smoked salmon and scrambled eggs turns breakfast into a special occasion, yet it's very quick and easy to make. A test of a hotel's breakfast is its scrambled eggs. At Morston, breakfast is often the last meal guests have to remember you by, so it's vital they're sent away with something delicious, no matter how delightful dinner might have been the night before. For this recipe use about 1lb salmon cut into thin steaks, about 1cm (½ inch) thick (avoid the tail end as it can be salty). If you have a good fishmonger ask him to slice it for you, otherwise do it yourself. We have chickens at home, so can make this breakfast with the freshest of eggs.

I. Pre-heat the grill to medium and place the slices of smoked salmon on to a grill pan or baking tray.

2. Gently whisk the eggs in a bowl, together with the nutmeg, a little salt and a good grinding of black pepper, then drop in the pieces of butter. Place the smoked salmon slices under the grill to just warm through.

3. Place the whisked eggs and butter in a heavy-based pan and heat gently over a moderate heat, stirring with a wooden spoon. As soon as the scrambled eggs start to come together, remove from the heat (they will continue to cook.

4. Place three slices of warmed smoked salmon across the centre of each plate, stir the chopped herbs into the cooked eggs and spoon over the top.

5. Serve with toasted and buttered spelt flour bread (see recipe on page 25).

Crumpets with Blueberry Butter

Crumpets may be more readily associated with teatime, served with clotted cream and jam, or as a dessert with a generous scoop of homemade ice cream, but I think they also make a very British breakfast. Pikelets, as my northern wife Tracy calls them, are a current favourite with our boys, Harry and Sam, as a breakfast treat. Both the crumpet batter and the blueberry butter can be made the night before and stored in the fridge. Believe it or not, although blueberries may sound like high-carbon-footprint import, they are actually grown by Peter Knights at King's Lynn, so qualify as a Norfolk ingredient!

1. To make the crumpet batter, pour the milk into a pan and heat until just warm. Stir in the sugar and yeast and leave to stand for 10 minutes until the milk starts to froth. Sift the flour and salt into a bowl, make a well in the centre, add the milk and beat until smooth.

2. Cover and leave in a warm place for 1 hour (or overnight) until doubled in size and full of air bubbles.

3. While the batter is resting, make the blueberry butter. Place the blueberries and sugar in a pan with two tablespoons water and simmer until syrupy. Leave to cool, then blitz in a blender until you have a rough purée. Place the butter in a bowl and whip until light, then fold through the blueberry mixture.

4. To make the crumpets, mix the bicarbonate of soda with 80ml (3fl oz) of water and beat this into the batter.

5. Lightly brush a large, heavy-based frying pan and 4 metal ring moulds, each 7.5cm (3 inches), with butter. Spoon approximately 3 tablespoons batter into each mould and cook over a low heat, for 6–7 minutes, until lots of bubbles have formed on the surface. Loosen the moulds and turn the crumpets over to cook the other side for 1–2 minutes.

6. Remove to a wire rack to cool a little before serving warm with a dollop of blueberry butter..

MAKES 8

For the crumpets
175ml (6fl oz) milk
3/4 tsp caster sugar
5g (1/4 oz) dried yeast
175g (6oz) plain flour
pinch of salt
1/4 tsp bicarbonate of soda

For the blueberry butter
110g (4oz) fresh blueberries
25g (1oz) caster sugar
110g (4oz) butter, softened, plus extra butter for brushing

Spelt Flour Bread with Sunflower, Sesame and Poppy Seeds

MAKES 1 X 900g (2LB) LOAF
450g (1lb) spelt flour
pinch of salt
25g (1oz) butter, softened
20g (3/4oz) caster sugar
40g (1 1/2oz) fresh yeast
1 large, free-range egg, lightly beaten
225ml (8fl oz) milk

For the topping
1 large, free-range egg, beaten with
2 tbsp milk to make an egg wash
1 tbsp each sunflower, sesame and
poppy seeds, mixed together

1 x 900g (2lb) loaf tin, greased and
lined with greaseproof paper

I am very pleased to see this traditional flour enjoying a revival, especially as the one we use is sourced locally from Letheringsett mill. We use it every day at Morston Hall. You can buy fresh yeast from bakers or the bread counter in supermarkets.

1. Place the flour, salt and softened butter in the bowl of a food mixer and, using the dough hook or 'K' beater, mix thoroughly.

2. Combine the sugar and yeast in a bowl. Mix with your fingertips so that the yeast breaks down and becomes smooth and almost liquid. Add the egg and milk, mixing together thoroughly.

3. With the machine still running, slowly add this mixture to the flour (you may not need to use all of the liquid). Allow the machine to knead the dough for 5–8 minutes, or until it comes away from the sides of the bowl and does not stick to your fingers.

4. Remove the bowl from the mixer and cover the dough with a clean, damp tea towel. Leave in a warm place for about 1 hour, or until the dough has doubled in volume.

5. Turn the dough out on to a lightly floured surface and knead well with the palm of your hand until smooth and pliable. Place the dough in the loaf tin and pat down gently. Set aside somewhere warm to prove again or until the dough has risen well above the top of the tin – this should take about 45 minutes.

6. Pre-heat the oven to 200°C/400°F/Gas mark 6.

7. When the dough has risen again, brush the top of the loaf with egg wash and scatter over the mixed seeds. Bake in the centre of the pre-heated oven for 20–25 minutes: the loaf should sound hollow when you tap your knuckles on the top.

8. Remove from the oven and leave to cool on a wire rack.

SPELT BREAD

We're all told to eat more fibre and breakfast-time can be a great opportunity to do so, as long as you steer clear of the croissants and white bread!

A great source of fibre is spelt, a grain similar to wheat. Dating from Roman times, it has been regarded for centuries as peasant food, and is still grown today in central Europe. Until recently it was seen as fairly worthy but has become fashionable for its huskiness and health benefits – it's mostly gluten free so suits all the people with wheat intolerance, although isn't suitable for coeliacs.

Spelt flour makes a coarse pale bread, similar in colour and in texture to light rye breads, but with a slightly sweet and nutty flavour. We get our spelt flour from Letheringsett, which is now the only working watermill in Norfolk – a century ago there would have been almost a hundred. Mike and Marion Thurlow bought the mill about twenty years ago and their business has evolved over the years much as we have at Morston – you can even visit and have a tour of the mill to see it in operation. Their flour is second to none: really versatile, too, as you can use it on its own or mixed with other flour.

Buttermilk Pancakes with Maple Syrup and Crispy Bacon

MAKES ABOUT 20 PANCAKES

175g (6oz) plain flour

1 tsp baking powder

1 large, free-range egg

about 225ml (8fl oz) buttermilk or full-fat milk

1 tbsp golden syrup

25g (1oz) butter, melted

oil or lard, for greasing

Served with maple syrup and crisp grilled bacon, these pancakes make a rather decadent breakfast dish. They're also a favourite with our children, although the bacon tends to get left off and replaced with more maple syrup! Any leftover batter can be used to make Scotch pancakes (also known as drop scones) for tea with jam and cream, served warm just to make them really difficult to eat! They're a popular teatime treat at Morston.

1. Place the flour and baking powder in a bowl, make a well in the centre then add the egg and half the milk. Beat to a smooth, thick batter, then beat in enough of the remaining milk to give the consistency of thick cream.

2. Warm the golden syrup a little, then beat this into the batter, along with the melted butter.

3. Heat a large, heavy-based, non-stick frying pan and lightly grease with oil or lard, wiping out any excess. Drop tablespoonfuls of the batter into the frying pan, spacing the mixture well apart. When bubbles start to appear on top, turn the pancakes and cook on the other side for a further 30 seconds to 1 minute until they are a light golden-brown.

4. Remove from the frying pan and place on a wire rack to cool, covering them with a tea towel to keep them soft. Grease the pan as before, and continue cooking until all the batter has been used up.

CRABS
PULL IN 20 YDS
AHEAD

I have little time for lunch during the week as I'm working at Morston, doing cookery demonstrations or filming for a television programme. But I do enjoy trying out the food in other restaurants, keeping abreast of trends and socialising at the same time.

If I'm going out to lunch I always look for something seasonal. Recently I had my perfect lunch: fresh sardines with crunchy lemon and breadcrumb (gremolata) topping, followed by a double loin lamb chop on the bone – simply cooked, but the lamb was pink. I'm not for overcomplicating and I don't like food to be masked with overpowering flavours. It's better if the basic ingredient can sing. Some bland ingredients such as tuna or squid can handle spices but it's a skilled hand that can complement food rather the complicate it. At lunchtime I also really enjoy a salad with radishes, crisp lettuce, French dressing, beetroot and new potatoes.

At home we rarely do formal lunches but we always do a roast on Sunday. We lead hectic lives so we need one day to relax as a family. Tracy's parents come round and so does my dad. The current favourite is pork with crackling and apple sauce.

On the subject of lunches, what children are eating at school is a real interest of mine. On the back of Jamie Oliver highlighting the state of school dinners, Norfolk County Services – which provide meals to three-hundred schools in the county – asked me to go into schools and talk to the children about food. It's one of the most fulfilling things I do – talking to four- to ten-year-olds about food – because they're all really interested. In fact, the more difficult the area, the better the response.

The problems come when the parents are there as they immediately put up barriers, saying 'the children won't eat that' and so on, but I find that children will try anything as long as you engage them in the process. We make things they can relate to – tomato ketchup, real fish fingers, mashed potato, real strawberry jelly … It's getting them cooking in some shape or form, which has to be a good thing.

The ninety minutes I'm in there has to be fun. Tracy dug out my old home economics report from school and my mark was very average – it said, 'Galton shows some potential in this subject if only he'd listen.' I remember the first thing I made at school was pineapple upside-down pudding!

Hazelnut-buttered Lamb Chops with Tomato Chutney

Much of this mouth-watering recipe can be made in advance: the hazelnut butter has to be chilled for at least three hours, while the tomato chutney keeps well in the fridge for a couple of days. Boiled new potatoes and lightly dressed salad leaves go well with this dish.

1. Pre-heat the grill to high.

2. To make the tomato chutney, place the garlic and chopped shallot onto a small baking tray. Cut a small cross in the top of each tomato then sit them on top of the garlic and shallot.

3. Drizzle with olive oil and season with salt and pepper then place under the pre-heated grill until the tomato skins start to blister. Peel off any charred skin, then place on a chopping board with the garlic and shallot and roughly chop everything.

4. Transfer the chopped tomatoes, garlic and shallot to a saucepan with all the remaining chutney ingredients, except for the coriander, and mix well. Bring to simmering point and reduce until slightly thickened; season with salt and pepper. When cool, chill until needed. Add the coriander just before serving.

5. Place the hazelnuts in a food processor and blitz briefly until finely chopped. Add the butter, herbs and garlic, season with salt and pepper and blitz again. Remove the mixture from the food processor and place on a work surface. Gather the mixture into a 'sausage' shape, about 13cm (5 inches) long and about 5cm (2 inches) in diameter. Wrap in clingfilm and place in the fridge to firm up for at least 3 hours.

6. Pre-heat the oven to 200°C/400°F/Gas mark 6.

7. Heat a large frying pan until hot, then add a little oil and a knob of butter. Place some of the chops in the hot pan and seal each one, turning them to colour well as you do so (you will need to do this in several batches, as it is important not to overcrowd the frying pan). Remove from the pan and set aside to cool.

8. Take the roll of hazelnut butter from the fridge, remove the clingfilm and slice into 18 rounds, each about 3mm (⅛ inch) thick. Press a disc of the topping firmly on to each chop.

9. Place the chops on a trivet in a roasting tin and roast in the pre-heated oven for 5 minutes. Allow to rest in a warm place for 5 minutes, then serve with the tomato chutney.

SERVES 6

For the tomato chutney

1 large garlic clove, peeled and halved
1 shallot, peeled and roughly chopped
4 large vine tomatoes
1 tbsp olive oil
1 large mild red chilli, finely chopped
1 tsp grated fresh ginger
a good pinch of crushed cumin seeds
2 tbsp fresh lime juice
1 tbsp soft dark brown sugar
1 tbsp red wine vinegar
3 tbsp chopped coriander

For the lamb chops

50g (2oz) toasted hazelnuts
75g (3oz) softened butter
1½ tbsp chopped mint
1½ tbsp chopped coriander
1 garlic clove, crushed
olive oil and butter for frying
18 best end of neck lamb chops
seasoning

Quick Cassoulet

What makes this dish summery – rather than the classic heavy, wintry French stew – is the addition of young carrots, new-season broad beans and sun-ripened tomatoes. OK, it's never going to be fast food, but my version of cassoulet is considerably quicker to put together than the traditional version, which involves a long cooking process.

The cassoulet still needs to be made well in advance (and the beans soaked overnight) but, by using pork fillet, the dish is finished quickly and easily. And, as Norfolk is pig-farming country – its dry, sunny climate is perfect for rearing high-quality meat – we always use excellent local pork for this dish.

SERVES 6

275g (10oz) dried haricot beans

100ml (4fl oz) olive oil

570ml (1 pint) chicken stock

3 vine tomatoes, peeled, deseeded and chopped

1 small onion, peeled and chopped

1 garlic clove, peeled and finely chopped

2 tbsp chopped parsley

1 tbsp snipped chives

3 pork fillets each weighing about 350g (12oz), trimmed of any sinew and fat

oil and butter for frying

6 rosemary sprigs

seasoning

1. Start making the cassoulet at least a day in advance by soaking the beans overnight in cold water.

2. Pour 25ml (1fl oz) olive oil into a saucepan, add the drained beans and sweat over a moderate heat for about 10 minutes. Add the chicken stock, bring to the boil and, with the lid on the saucepan, simmer gently for about 45 minutes until the beans are soft. Drain the beans again, reserving the stock you cooked them in, and set aside.

3. Return the stock to the saucepan, bring to the boil and reduce by at least half. Add the tomatoes, onion, garlic, beans and remaining 75ml (3fl oz) olive oil, bring back to the boil for a further 5 minutes, taste and season and set aside.

4. Pre-heat the oven to 200°C/400°F/Gas mark 6.

5. To cook the pork fillets, heat a non-stick frying pan until hot; add a splash of olive oil followed by a knob of butter. Seal the pork fillets, turning them to colour on all sides. Transfer to a trivet in a roasting tin, season well and place 2 sprigs of rosemary on top of each fillet. Roast in the oven for 15–20 minutes, depending on their thickness.

6. Remove from the oven and allow to rest somewhere warm for a few minutes. Reheat the cassoulet and stir in the herbs. Place some cassoulet in the centre of each plate and carve slices of the pork fillet on top.

NORFOLK PORK

Norfolk has a dry climate – a bit of a microclimate really – so is ideal for pig farming, which doesn't suit wet conditions. The countryside is also quite flat in places, which is another advantage when you're trying to put up a pig pen! Pork features in many guises at Morston, from black pudding, scrumptious sausages and bacon at breakfast to wonderfully succulent, flavourful pork fillet, as used in my summery cassoulet recipe

Look for a dark, dry skin when buying pork for roasting as this will give you the best crackling – some people rub it with oil before cooking, but I prefer to add a splash of water and some salt. It's a shame people don't eat more pork, as these days it's a lot less fatty than it used to be so is a healthier choice. I believe passionately in sourcing as much of our food as possible locally, so most of our meat comes from Arthur Howell, who has shops in Wells, Burnham Market and Binham, as well as his own abattoir so we know exactly how the meat is butchered. It also means we know how long the meat has been hung for, which is particularly crucial as it adds depth of flavour and soft texture.

HOMEMADE LAVENDER BREAD

fresh Pasta sauce

Local Rare breed pork pies with caramelised onion marmalade

Homemade Cakes

SAMPHIRE

Crab Spring Rolls with Broad Bean, Asparagus and Pea Relish

SERVES 6

For the relish

a good pinch of sugar

75g (3oz) broad beans

75g (3oz) asparagus tips

75g (3oz) frozen petits pois

1 tbsp mayonnaise

fresh lime juice

seasoning

For the spring rolls

6 dressed crabs

100g (3½ oz) fresh beansprouts

1 small can sweetcorn kernels, drained

zest of ½ lime

2 tbsp chopped fresh coriander

12 sheets filo pastry (or spring roll wrappers)

125g (4½ oz) butter, melted

oil for frying

seasoning

I may be biased, but in my opinion Cromer crabs are the best, with a sweeter flavour and less fibrous texture than the much larger Cornish crabs, which to me tend to lose their flavour as they get bigger. But I would say this as I'm from Norfolk! These moreish spring rolls are served with a really flavoursome and vibrant relish. Spring rolls may sound as if they are difficult to make, but in fact this recipe couldn't be easier. The relish can be made up to two days ahead, covered tightly with clingfilm and stored in the fridge.

1. Make the relish first: bring a saucepan of lightly salted water to the boil, add a good pinch of sugar and throw in the broad beans, asparagus tips and peas. Cook until just tender then drain, retaining the water you cooked them in.

2. Place broad beans, asparagus and peas in a blender and add 4 tablespoons of the hot water they were cooked in. Blitz to a vibrant green purée, pour into a bowl and allow to cool. Mix in the mayonnaise and a good squeeze of lime juice and season well with salt and pepper. Chill until needed.

3. For the spring rolls, place the crab meat, beansprouts, sweetcorn, lime zest and chopped coriander in a bowl. Using your hands, mix well until fairly firm. Check the seasoning and set aside.

4. Lay a piece of filo pastry on the work surface (covering the rest with a damp tea towel to prevent them from drying out) and brush with melted butter. Spoon one-twelfth of the mixture near the edge of the filo pastry closest to you, then carefully roll the filo pastry up tightly into a cigar shape, folding in the sides as you go. Brush again with melted butter. Repeat to make 12 parcels.

5. Shallow-fry the spring rolls in a wok or frying pan, turning to colour all over, then drain well on kitchen paper. Serve hot with the relish.

Monkfish and Mango Kebabs with Spicy Salsa

I like to cook these on a barbecue because monkfish is a meaty fish and lends itself well to this cooking method – unlike softer, flakier fish, it doesn't break up as it cooks – but they could also be roasted in the oven. Get the children to help thread the pieces on to the skewers. The salsa can also be made in advance; if you do this, press clingfilm directly on to it and add another layer tightly over the bowl to prevent the avocado from discolouring. It will keep overnight in the fridge.

SERVES 6

For the kebabs

3 monkfish tails, taken off the bone and membrane removed

grated zest of 1 lime

good splash of olive oil

2 ripe mangoes

1 courgette

1 red pepper

1 x 20g pack fresh basil

seasoning

thick Greek yoghurt, to serve

1. Cube the monkfish and place it in a large bowl together with the lime zest. Season with salt and pepper, pour over a good splash of olive oil, mix well and set aside.

You will also need 6 wooden kebab skewers, pre-soaked in water if cooking on the barbecue.

2. Peel the mangoes and cut the flesh into large cubes, slice the courgette quite chunkily and cut the pepper into squares. Remove the basil leaves from the stalks.

3. Thread a cube of monkfish on to a kebab skewer, followed by a cube of mango, a slice of courgette, a square of pepper and a basil leaf. Repeat the process until all the ingredients are used up and place the kebabs in the fridge until you are ready to cook them.

4. Make sure the barbecue is hot and ready or pre-heat the oven to 200°C/400°F/Gas mark 6.

5. Cook the kebabs on the barbecue for about 5 minutes on each side or roast in the pre-heated oven for 8-10 minutes. Serve with a good blob of Greek yoghurt on top of the spicy salsa (see next page).

For the salsa

2 red peppers, halved lengthways

2 red chillies, halved lengthways and seeds removed

2 garlic cloves, peeled and halved

olive oil

1 ripe avocado, peeled and diced

juice of 1 lime

2 tomatoes, peeled, deseeded and chopped

1/2 small cucumber, diced

1 small red onion, peeled and chopped

3 tbsp thick Greek yoghurt

bunch of coriander, chopped

seasoning

Spicy Salsa

1. Pre-heat the oven to 200°C/400°F/Gas mark 6.

2. Place the peppers on a roasting tray, cut side facing upwards; season with salt and pepper. Place half a chilli and half a garlic clove in each pepper and douse well with olive oil.

3. Roast in the pre-heated oven until the peppers begin to soften and the skins start to blister and peel. Remove to a bowl, cover with clingfilm and leave to cool.

4. When cool enough to handle, slip off the skins. Chop the peppers, chillies and garlic and place in a bowl with all the remaining salsa ingredients. Mix thoroughly, seasoning with salt and pepper.

Free-range Chicken Breasts with Satay Sauce

This is another dish that is good for entertaining as the sauce can be made well in advance and the chicken breasts prepared, ready to cook when your guests arrive. Buy free-range chicken breasts if you can as the flavour is so much better.

1. Begin by making the satay sauce: place the coconut cream and hot water in a bowl and stir well to melt, then add the peanut butter and mix thoroughly to combine. Add all the remaining ingredients, mix well to make a fairly thick sauce, season and set aside.

2. Using a sharp knife, cut the under fillet away from each chicken breast and then slice the breasts lengthways into 3 strips (you will end up with four pieces of chicken per breast). Place the chicken in a bowl with the chopped parsley or coriander, lemon zest and juice and the sunflower oil. Season with salt and pepper then mix well. Cover the bowl with clingfilm and place in the fridge to marinate for at least an hour, preferably overnight.

3. Pre-heat the oven to 180°C/350°F/Gas mark 4.

4. Heat a non-stick frying pan and, when it is hot, add the chicken strips (you may need to do this in batches to avoid overcrowding the pan). Fry them quickly, turning to colour and seal them all over. Transfer to a roasting tin and roast in the pre-heated oven for 10 minutes.

5. Serve the chicken with a little satay sauce spooned over and sprinkled with spring onions.

SERVES 6

For the sauce

50g (2oz) creamed coconut
6 tbsp hot water
125g (4½oz) crunchy peanut butter
good pinch of turmeric
3 tbsp finely chopped shallot
3 tbsp light soy sauce
1 tsp finely grated root ginger
1 large mild red chilli, seeds removed and finely chopped
seasoning

For the chicken breasts

6 free-range chicken breasts, skin removed
3 tbsp chopped parsley or coriander
grated zest and juice of ½ lemon
4 tbsp sunflower oil
seasoning
4 spring onions, peeled and finely sliced, to serve

Spiced Sea Bream with Cucumber Relish

Sea bream – a fairly small rounded fish which will serve two people as a starter – has a similar taste to sea bass. Sea bass or mackerel would work just as well for this recipe if you can't find bream. And don't worry if you're unable to find all the spices – the fish will be just as delicious using whatever spices are readily available. In addition to the cucumber relish, you can serve this on a bed of tomato chutney – see page 38 for the recipe. To pinbone the fillets, simply pull out the centre bones along the back with a pair of tweezers.

SERVES 6

3 whole sea bream, skinned, filleted and pinboned

100g (3½oz) plain flour

1 tbsp cornflour

¼ tsp garam masala powder

¼ tsp chilli powder

¼ tsp ground turmeric

¼ tsp ground coriander

2 garlic cloves

1 large knob of fresh root ginger, about 2.5cm (1 inch)

vegetable oil for deep-frying

seasoning

For the cucumber relish

1 cucumber, peeled, deseeded and cut into wafer-thin strips

2 tomatoes, skinned, deseeded and cut into strips

½ red onion, peeled and cut into thin strips

bunch of coriander leaves, very roughly chopped

juice of ½ lime

2 tbsp olive oil

seasoning

1. In a large bowl, mix all the dry ingredients together. Then, using a fine microplane grater, grate the garlic and ginger into a separate bowl. Mix the contents of both bowls together.

2. When you are ready to fry the fish, add 225ml (8fl oz) water and a little salt. Mix well.

3. Pour vegetable oil into a deep-sided pan to a depth of about 5cm (2 inches). Place over a moderate heat and bring up to a temperature of about 140–160°C (275–320°F); if you don't have a thermometer, test the temperature of the oil by dropping in a little batter. If it rises straight to the top and fries then the temperature is correct.

4. Dip the sea bream fillets into the batter, turning them until thoroughly coated, then gently lower them into the oil. Fry for about 3 minutes, then carefully remove from the oil and drain on kitchen paper; season with salt and pepper.

5. You can then either bring the oil back up to temperature and re-fry the fish to serve immediately or leave them for an hour then re-fry. Either way, drain the fish thoroughly on kitchen paper before serving immediately on a bed of tomato chutney if you like (see recipe page 38), together with some cucumber relish, made by mixing all the ingredients together in a bowl, seasoning and serving immediately.

Cod Fritters with Chilli Tomato Sauce

We're fortunate in Norfolk to get our cod straight out of the North Sea, line-caught rather than netted so the fish are in better condition and not bruised from being dragged along by nets. But cod from the supermarket is fine. You can part-cook the fish an hour before using so that a quick dip back in the hot oil is all that is needed to serve.

SERVES 6

For batter mix

125g (4½oz) plain flour
½ tsp baking powder
½ tsp bicarbonate of soda
50g (2oz) cornflour
a little ground coriander (optional)
pinch of ground cumin
225ml (8 fl oz) cold lager
seasoning

For the chilli tomato sauce

8 decent-sized vine tomatoes
2 large red chillies, sliced lengthways and deseeded
2 garlic cloves, peeled and chopped
1 small onion or shallot, peeled and sliced
5cm (2 inch) nugget of fresh root ginger, peeled and sliced
1 tbsp dark soft brown sugar
1 thyme sprig, leaves removed
65ml (2½fl oz) olive oil
squeeze of fresh lemon juice
seasoning

6 decent-sized fillets of line-caught cod, each 75-110g (3-4oz), pinboned and skinned
vegetable oil for shallow-frying
seasoned flour

1. To make the dry batter, mix all the ingredients except for the lager in a bowl, season with salt and pepper and store until needed.

2. Pre-heat the grill to high.

3. To make the chilli tomato sauce, cut a small cross in the top of each tomato and place on the grill pan with the chillies. Scatter over the garlic, onion, ginger, brown sugar and leaves from the thyme.

4. Place under the grill until the tomatoes have softened and the skins charred a little. Blitz the whole lot in a liquidiser and push through a fine sieve into a bowl. Add the oil, a little fresh lemon juice and salt and pepper to taste. Set aside to use later.

5. When you are ready to cook the fish, place the prepared dry batter mix into a bowl, pour in the lager all at once and quickly mix, using a fork; it's fine if there are a few lumps in the mixture as this will produce a lighter batter. Spread the seasoned flour on to a plate.

6. Pour vegetable oil into a deep-sided saucepan to a depth of about 5cm (2 inches). Place over a moderate heat and bring up to a temperature of about 140–160°C (275–320°F); if you don't have a thermometer, test the temperature of the oil by dropping in a little batter. If it rises straight to the top and fries then the temperature is correct.

7. Dip each cod fillet into the seasoned flour to coat, then shake off any excess before dipping them into the batter mix to coat well. Carefully drop each coated piece of fish into the hot oil (it is better not to do a lot at one time otherwise the temperature of the oil will drop too much). Turn each piece of fish over and, as soon as they are very lightly coloured, carefully remove with a slotted spoon and place on kitchen paper to drain.

8. You can then either bring the oil back up to temperature and re-fry the fish to serve immediately or leave them for an hour then re-fry. Either way, drain the fish thoroughly on kitchen paper before serving with warmed chilli tomato sauce.

Lobster, Crab and Avocado Cocktail with Sweetcorn Ice Cream

If I could eat lobster every day I'd be happy! Ours are caught off Morston by Willie Weston, a great character from Blakeney. This modern take on an old-fashioned British dish is a million miles from a glass of shredded lettuce with three prawns lurking inside, swamped with 'Marie Rose' sauce. It may appear that there are a lot of ingredients here but the preparation can all be done in advance, leaving you to assemble the cocktail when you are ready. I like to use large glasses for serving this, but glass bowls would also be fine. It may sound strange to serve ice cream with a savoury dish, but a little blob of sweetcorn ice cream complements the sweetness of the lobster and crab flesh beautifully.

1. To make the dressing, begin by picking the brown crab meat over carefully to make sure there is no shell or cartilage left in, then weigh out 125g (4½oz), reserving the rest. Place the 125g (4½oz) brown crab meat, tomato ketchup, Tabasco and Worcestershire sauces, paprika and lime juice in a bowl and mix thoroughly, adding and tasting as you go along to achieve the flavour you want. Then add enough mayonnaise for the required consistency and season to taste. Once you are happy with the dressing cover with clingfilm and set aside in the fridge.

2. For the cocktail, remove all the meat from the lobsters (not forgetting to crack the claws and get all the claw meat out), break it up a little and place in a bowl.

3. Place the new potatoes in a pan of cold, salted water, add the mint, bring to the boil and cook until tender. Drain and refresh under cold running water, chop the potatoes and set aside.

4. To assemble the dish; place shredded lettuce into the bottom of each glass, divide the lobster meat into 6 portions and place this on top of the lettuce. To each glass, add a little chopped cucumber and some white and brown crab meat. Top this with a couple of grapefruit segments, avocados, some pieces of cooked potato and hard-boiled egg.

5. To finish, spoon over some dressing and sprinkle with chives. Serve immediately with a small bowl of Sweetcorn Ice Cream (see recipe p54).

SERVES 6

For the dressing
125g (4oz) brown crab meat, from the dressed crabs (see below)
1 tbsp tomato ketchup
good splash of Tabasco sauce
good splash of Worcestershire sauce
good pinch of paprika
juice of 1 lime
home-made mayonnaise or good-quality bought
seasoning

For the lobster, crab and avocado cocktail
3 small cooked lobsters, each about 450g (1lb)
6 small new potatoes, scrubbed
a couple of fresh mint sprigs
2 Little Gem lettuces, shredded
½ cucumber, peeled, deseeded and chopped
3 large dressed crabs, white and brown meat separated
1 pink grapefruit, peeled and segmented
2 ripe avocados, peeled and chopped
3 free-range eggs, hardboiled and quartered
2 tbsp snipped fresh chives

Sweetcorn Ice Cream

For the ice cream
6 tbsp white wine
60g (2½oz) caster sugar
juice of 1 lemon
6 sweetcorn cobs
120ml (4fl oz) milk
salt

I can see eyebrows being raised at the idea of sweetcorn ice cream but, trust me, it really does go well with shellfish. You don't have to have an ice-cream machine to make good ice cream: the mixture can be frozen in a deep-sided plastic container, removing it from the freezer every 20 minutes to give it a good whisk until it is completely firm.

1. Place the white wine, sugar and lemon juice in a pan over a low heat with 100ml (3½fl oz) water. Heat gently until the sugar has melted.

2. Strip the kernels from the cob and add to the saucepan. Bring to the boil and simmer over a moderate heat for about 5 minutes until the sweetcorn is cooked. Remove from the heat, then blitz the whole lot in a liquidiser, adding the milk as you do so. Pass through a sieve into a jug, taste and season with a little salt if needed, then leave to cool.

3. Churn in an ice-cream machine (or by hand, see above) then store in a suitable container in the freezer for up to a month.

Crisp Shrimp Risotto Cakes

This recipe really came about from wondering what to do with some leftover risotto as I hate to see food wasted. So you could make a double quantity of this risotto, eat it freshly made the first day then the following day make a batch of the wonderful crisp risotto cakes. I prefer to use brown shrimps for this as they have a lovely sweet depth of flavour and are available locally, although little pink shrimps, or Morecambe Bay shrimps, also work nicely too.

1. To make the risotto, heat the chicken stock over a low heat. Meanwhile, in a large pan, melt the butter and gently sauté the shallots and garlic. Add the rice and, stirring continuously, cook for a few minutes until it glistens and is well coated with butter.

2. Add the white wine and cook until evaporated. Start stirring in the hot stock, a ladleful at a time, adding the next one only when most of the stock has been absorbed (don't try to rush it as time is of the essence for a really successful risotto). You may not need to use all the stock, but it's better to have it ready just in case.

3. When the risotto is creamy in texture but not chalky, and the grains still retain some 'bite', stir in the brown shrimps and petits pois, making sure they are warmed right through.

4. Finally, stir in the Parmesan, followed by the chives. Season to taste. Ladle the risotto into bowls and serve immediately.

For the crisp risotto cakes

1. Place the egg wash and breadcrumbs into separate shallow bowls.

2. Take the cold risotto, loosen with a little hot water, then divide the mixture into 12. Using your hands, form even-sized slightly flattened fishcakes about 1cm (½ inch) thick. Dip each risotto cake into the egg wash, then the breadcrumbs, making sure they are lightly and evenly coated. Place the finished risotto cakes on a tray lined with greaseproof paper, cover with clingfilm and keep in the fridge until needed.

3. To cook the risotto cakes, heat a large, heavy-based frying pan over a medium heat and, once hot, add a splash of olive oil. Fry the risotto cakes gently for about 4 minutes on each side until well coloured and warmed right through. Serve with a tomato salad.

SERVES 6

1.2 litres (2 pints) chicken or vegetable stock

50g (2oz) salted butter

2 shallots, peeled and finely chopped

2 garlic cloves, peeled and chopped

250g (9oz) risotto rice, preferably Arborio

4 tbsp white wine

250g (9oz) peeled shrimps, preferably brown

75g (3oz) fresh or frozen petits pois

50g (2oz) finely grated fresh Parmesan

3 tbsp finely snipped fresh chives

seasoning

1 egg whisked with 6 tbsp milk to make an egg wash

breadcrumbs (for a really crisp crust, use freeze-dried Japanese crumbs if you can get them)

olive oil, for frying

tomato salad, to serve

What could be more quintessentially British than afternoon tea – that wonderful interlude between lunch and dinner when the sun's rays start to lengthen and it's time to put the kettle on for a reviving cuppa?

At Morston, tea is a sumptuous affair – laid out in the light, spacious surroundings of the elegant conservatory overlooking the garden: smoked salmon sandwiches (with the crusts off, of course!), china pots of loose tea and plates of neat little scones served with homemade jam and lashings of real clotted cream.

It's lovely to go out and have a really brilliant afternoon tea. My ultimate sandwich would be my triple decker sandwich – the recipe is in this book – which has layers of egg mayonnaise and cress, smoked salmon, and cucumber and cream cheese … everything in one delicate sandwich! It's also very neat: you don't want doorstep wedges but something quite sophisticated.

A really good afternoon tea should be sought after and special. I have a very sweet tooth, so cakes really hit the spot – éclairs or little meringues filled with cream and passion fruit curd; anything that sticks to the teeth! I'm not overly keen on very rich fruit cakes but I love a moist chocolate cake. The one in this book – chocolate soufflé cake – came about after a disaster when Tracy made it at home. She followed a recipe that didn't work but it turned out to be really good and gooey.

My mother used to make a cake at least once a week – there were five of us boys to feed! My favourite was a lemon curd cake. Mums were good cooks then because they were generally housewives so had the time to cook properly – to cook well, you definitely need time.

The Best Triple Decker Sandwich

SERVES 6

1 loaf multi-seeded bread

1 loaf good-quality white bread

softened butter for spreading

6 wafer-thin slices smoked salmon (about 300g/11oz)

juice of 1 lime

3 hard-boiled eggs

1 large tbsp homemade or good-quality bought mayonnaise

1 small punnet mustard cress

splash of anchovy essence (optional)

small carton of cream cheese

1/2 cucumber, peeled and sliced lengthways as thin as possible (use a potato peeler)

seasoning

A really good afternoon tea is a part of British tradition that should still be held in the highest regard, and the idea of this triple decker sandwich is that it takes all the components of classic teatime sandwiches – salmon, cucumber, egg – and puts them into one. Make sure you use really fresh bread and slice it very thinly. You can make these ahead of time, then cover with clingfilm and a lightly dampened tea towel.

1. Cut 12 slices of brown bread and 12 slices of white bread really thinly. Spread the brown bread with butter on one side, then lay 6 slices of brown bread side by side in a flat rectangle on a work surface.

2. Cover with the smoked salmon slices and season with pepper and a good squeeze of lime juice. Cover the salmon with 6 slices of white bread, buttered on both sides. In a bowl, use a fork to mash the eggs with the mayonnaise, mustard cress, anchovy essence (if using) and a good seasoning of salt and pepper. Spread this mixture over the buttered white bread to create your second layer of filling. Cover with the remaining buttered brown bread.

3. Spread the brown bread with cream cheese to create your third filling. Cover with long slices of cucumber, then season lightly with salt and pepper. Butter the remaining 6 slices of white bread and place these, buttered side down, on top of the cucumber, pressing down firmly all over. Using a serrated knife, cut off the crusts and cut into finger-sized sandwiches.

Easy Setting Strawberry and Elderflower Jam

In Britain, the hedgerows are full of elderflowers during May and June, which is also the time that home-grown strawberries are at their best, so this really is a food marriage made in heaven. Strawberries and elderflowers are one of those glorious examples of food combinations in season at the same time: think blackberries and apples, mint and new potatoes, lobster and samphire. At Morston, whenever we get a good crop of seasonal fruit, homemade jam is invariably produced (see page 197 for details of my mail-order preserves). Strawberry is probably my favourite; the addition of elderflowers gives a wonderful extra dimension and makes this jam a bit different, but of course, if the elderflower season is over, you can just leave them out. Make sure you pick elderflowers away from the road, to avoid polluted blossoms.

MAKES 1.35kg (3lb)

900g (2lb) hulled strawberries, cut in half if large

900g (2lb) jam sugar with added pectin

4 good heads of elderflowers, washed and tied in a piece of muslin

juice of ½ lemon

1. Place the strawberries, sugar and elderflowers in a large preserving pan. Stir well with a wooden spoon and heat gently until the sugar has melted. Turn the heat up to high and, when it reaches boiling point, time it for 5 minutes, skimming off any scum that rises to the surface.

2. Test to see if the jam has reached setting point by dropping some on to a cold plate; if it ripples when you draw your finger through it, then the setting stage has been reached. Remove from the heat immediately, take out the elderflower heads, stir in the lemon juice and allow to cool in the pan.

3. When the jam has cooled, carefully ladle into sterilised jars, cover and seal immediately.

Quick and Easy Lemon and Lime Curd Tartlets

MAKES 12-16

For the pastry:

150g (5oz) plain flour, sifted

25g (1oz) caster sugar

pinch of salt

75g (3oz) softened unsalted butter

1 egg yolk, beaten with 1 tbsp milk

For the lemon and lime curd:

150g (5oz) caster sugar

4 eggs

grated zest and juice of 1 large lemon

grated zest of 1 lime, plus the juice of 3 limes

2 elderflower heads (optional)

125g (4½oz) unsalted butter

The lemon and lime curd used to fill these tarts is very easy to make, keeps in the fridge for over a month and is wonderfully fresh and zingy, whether you use it for tartlets or on hot, buttered toast! The amount given makes quite a lot of curd but it's a good idea to have a couple of jars in the fridge as a standby filling, especially as it keeps so well. These tartlets could be topped with meringue, fresh sliced mango or fresh raspberries.

1. Place the flour, sugar, salt and butter into a food processor and, using a pulse action, blitz until it forms the consistency of breadcrumbs. Add the egg-yolk-and-milk mixture and pulse again until it forms dough. Turn the dough out on to a lightly floured work surface and bring it together with your hands, then wrap in clingfilm and place in the fridge to rest for at least an hour.

2. Meanwhile, make the lemon and lime curd: in a bowl, whisk together the sugar, eggs, zest and juice of the lemon and limes, plus the elderflowers (if using). Place the bowl over a pan of simmering water and stir continuously for up to 15 minutes, until the mixture thickens. Remove from the heat and beat in the butter. Pass through a sieve into another bowl and set aside to cool.

3. Once the pastry has rested, remove it from the fridge and work it well with your hands to make it quite pliable. On a lightly floured work surface roll it out as thin as you dare then, using a pastry cutter, cut out rounds to fit into small Yorkshire pudding trays or bun trays. Press the pastry rounds into the Yorkshire pudding trays, line with greaseproof paper (or cupcake cases) and fill with baking beans. Return to the fridge to rest for a further 30 minutes.

4. Pre-heat the oven to 180°C/350°F/Gas mark 4.

5. Place the pastry cases into the pre-heated oven for about 15 minutes, then carefully remove the baking beans and greaseproof paper and bake for a further 5 minutes, until golden. Remove from the oven and allow to cool before spooning in liberal amounts of the lemon and lime curd.

Meringues with Peaches and Passion Fruit Jam

I have a very sweet tooth, so cakes of all kinds really hit the button for me! Peaches and meringue are just about perfect together.

1. Pre-heat the oven to 150°C/300°F/Gas mark 2.

2. Put the egg whites in a spotlessly clean bowl and, using an electric beater, whisk at high speed until soft peaks form. Still whisking, slowly add the caster sugar. Using a metal spoon, fold in the icing sugar and cornflour, then briskly beat in the lemon juice.

3. Place spoonfuls of the mixture on to a baking sheet covered with silicone-coated greaseproof paper, then make a well with a smaller spoon to form little meringue 'nests'. Place in the pre-heated oven for 1½ hours, then turn off the oven and leave the meringue nests in the oven until completely cold.

4. While the meringues are in the oven, place all the passion fruit jam ingredients into a pan and, over a low heat, allow the sugar to melt. Turn the heat up and boil to reduce a little (the consistency should be that of a fairly thick sauce). Remove from the heat and allow to cool.

5. When ready to serve, whip the cream to soft peaks. Fill each meringue nest with whipped cream, cover with peach slices and spoon over some passion fruit jam.

SERVES 6-8

6 egg whites
225g (8oz) caster sugar
110g (4oz) icing sugar
1 tbsp cornflour
juice of ½ lemon
6 really ripe peaches, peeled and sliced
425ml (15fl oz) double cream

For the passion fruit jam:
pulp and seeds from 12 passion fruit
75g (3oz) caster sugar
juice of 1 orange

EGGS

From eggs mingled with salad cress and mayo in the very best sandwiches à la Ritz, to newly laid eggs used for cakes, biscuits and other treats, the humble egg is an integral ingredient in the teatime chapter. We have about a dozen Bantams at home and Sam, our younger son, has taken to collecting their eggs every day before school, then charging me to buy them off him!

Eggs feature in almost every cake you bake, so it's well worth seeking out free-range ones where possible for the best taste. The freshness of the egg is particularly important when making mayonnaise or Hollandaise sauce as it really makes the end result something special, but it's also a good idea to use the freshest eggs for breakfast treats such as scrambled eggs.

You can always tell how fresh an egg is by the consistency of the white – if it's runny and liquid the egg is quite stale, but when fresh the egg white will surround the yolk and be more viscous in texture.

One of my favourite ways to cook eggs is by scrambling them. I like them runny and buttery; there's nothing better with hot, buttered toast!

PYO

STRAWBS

£3.70 per Kilo

CURRANTS

3.50 per kilo

RASPS

£4.60 per kilo

Real Raspberry Jelly

I think it's the deep pink colour and the massive hit of raspberry flavour that makes this jelly so good. Jelly seems to be making a bit of a fashionable comeback at the moment, with sweet and savoury jellies making an appearance everywhere. They're no longer the domain of the children's party. The sugar or stock syrup used to make this jelly is one of those standbys we always have in the fridge as it keeps well for up to a week. Once you have made up a quantity, use it for sorbets or for poaching fruit. You can omit the vanilla pod if you wish

SERVES 8

For the sugar (stock) syrup:
225g (8oz) caster sugar
1 vanilla pod, split (optional)
juice of 1/2 lemon

For the jelly:
700g (1 1/2 lb) really ripe English raspberries
275ml (1/2 pint) sugar (stock) syrup
4 gelatine leaves
fresh raspberries, to serve

1. First, make the sugar syrup: put the sugar and 425ml (3/4 pint) water into a pan. Scrape the seeds from the vanilla pod then add these to the sugar and water. Over a low heat, allow the sugar to dissolve then bring it up to a light simmer for 10 minutes. Remove from the heat and allow to cool, then stir in the lemon juice.

2. To make the jelly, place the raspberries and 275ml (1/2 pint) sugar (stock) syrup in a pan and gently bring to the boil. Poach the fruit slowly until it is really soft, then pass the mixture through a piece of muslin or jelly bag into a measuring jug (you should have about 570ml/1 pint liquid). Place the gelatine leaves into a tray of cold water for a few minutes to soften.

3. Remove the softened gelatine from the water, squeezing out any excess water with your hands as you do so, and stir it into the hot raspberry liquid (if it has cooled down already, heat a little in a small pan, stir in the softened gelatine leaves until dissolved, then stir into the rest of the juice). Pour into a jelly mould or 8 individual ramekins and place in the fridge, preferably overnight, to set.

4. Serve with fresh raspberries.

Vanilla Macaroons with Raspberry Filling

You will find these little delights difficult to resist once you have tasted one. A good macaroon should have a glossy or shiny top, a soft centre and a generous filling, sandwiched together, though at home I'm not overly bothered with visual perfection, only the flavour! It might take a bit of practice to get a perfect round with a glossy top, but they'll be delicious whatever they look like. I haven't specified a serving quantity for this recipe as it depends on the size of macaroons that you make.

1. To make the macaroons, line a baking sheet with good-quality greaseproof paper and set aside. Sift the icing sugar and almonds into a bowl. Place the egg whites into the bowl of an electric food mixer and whisk until they form stiff peaks. Whisk the vanilla extract into the egg whites, then gradually whisk in the caster sugar and continue to whisk until stiff and glossy.

2. Fold in the almonds and icing sugar gently until smooth (it will become quite runny, but this is fine). Put the mixture in a piping bag fitted with a plain 5mm (¼ inch) nozzle and pipe macaroons of the required size on to the greaseproof paper. Leave to rest for 10–15 minutes to allow the surface to become dry.

3. Pre-heat the oven to 150°C/300°F/Gas mark 2.

4. Bake for about 25 minutes (depending on size) – the macaroons are done when you can lift them off the baking sheet. Remove from the oven and leave to cool on the baking sheet.

5. While the macaroons are in the oven, make the raspberry filling by mixing all the ingredients together thoroughly, adding a little more sugar or raspberry purée to taste.

6. When the macaroons are completely cold, sandwich them with the filling and serve with fresh raspberries and a blob of vanilla ice cream.

For the macaroons:
175g (6oz) icing sugar
75g (3oz) ground almonds
75g (3oz) egg whites
½ tsp vanilla extract
25g (1oz) caster sugar
fresh raspberries and vanilla ice cream, to serve

For the raspberry filling:
250g tub mascarpone cheese
1 tbsp icing sugar
2 drops vanilla extract
5 tbsp raspberry purée, made from fresh raspberries pushed through a sieve

Passion Fruit Sponge Cake

Having spent some time cooking in Cape Town, where passion fruit is picked off the trees as here we would pick an apple, I have become quite blasé about using this tropical treat in my recipes. The flavour of passion fruit is second to none, and although it's an unusual curd that may not be associated with a traditional British sponge, you'll discover that it works really well.

I. Preheat the oven to 170°C/325°F/Gas mark 3.

2. Cream the butter and sugar together in a bowl till light and fluffy (an electric hand mixer is good for this). While continuing to whisk, slowly add the beaten eggs, orange zest and juice. Finally, using a metal spoon or spatula, fold in the flour, making sure it is thoroughly incorporated.

3. Spoon the mixture into the prepared tin, place it on the centre shelf of the pre-heated oven and bake for 40–50 minutes: the sponge is cooked when it is just starting to come away from the edges of the tin and the centre springs back when touched with a finger. Remove from the oven and turn out on to a wire rack to cool.

4. While the cake is in the oven, place all the passion fruit curd ingredients in a bowl and whisk well. Place the bowl over a pan of simmering water and stir continuously until the mixture becomes thick and creamy. Remove from the heat and allow to cool.

5. When the sponge is completely cold, cut it in half horizontally and spread the passion fruit curd over the bottom half. Sandwich the two halves together and dust with icing sugar to serve.

For the cake:
175g (6oz) softened unsalted butter
175g (6oz) caster sugar
3 eggs, beaten
zest and juice of 1/2 orange
175g (6oz) self-raising flour
icing sugar, to dust

For the passion fruit curd:
about 7 passion fruit (enough to make 150ml (1/4 pint) passion fruit pulp, including the pips)
75g (3oz) caster sugar
2 eggs
50g (2oz) unsalted butter

1 x 20cm (8 inch) cake tin, base and sides lined with good-quality greaseproof paper.

Chocolate Soufflé Cake

Everybody loves a sticky chocolate sponge, and this one is so sticky you need a fork to eat it with! Serve with whipped cream or crème fraiche or, alternatively, as a pudding with ice cream and strawberries. Either way, you've got to have a go as it is really good. Make sure you don't overcook it: to get some stickiness it needs to come out of the oven earlier rather than later.

SERVES 6

225g (8oz) butter

225g (8oz) good-quality plain chocolate, minimum 64% cocoa solids

1 tsp vanilla extract

5 eggs, separated

125g (4¼oz) caster sugar

110g (4oz) plain flour, sifted

75g (3oz) finely chopped walnuts

whipped cream or crème fraiche, to serve

1 x 900g (2lb) loaf tin or a round 20cm (8 inch) cake tin, lined with good-quality greaseproof paper.

l. Pre-heat the oven to 170°C/325°F/Gas mark 3.

2. Place the butter, chocolate and vanilla in a bowl over a pan of barely simmering water. Allow to melt (making sure the bottom of the bowl does not touch the water), then remove from the pan and allow to cool a little.

3. Whisk the egg yolks and the sugar together in a bowl until pale and creamy. Carefully pour the melted chocolate-and-butter mixture into the creamed egg yolks and mix well with a wooden spoon. Next, using a metal spoon, fold in the flour and chopped walnuts, making sure that everything is incorporated.

4. In another bowl, whisk the egg whites to form soft peaks, then take a small amount of this and beat vigorously into the chocolate mixture. Carefully fold in the remaining egg whites with a metal spoon until fully incorporated.

5. Pour the mixture into the prepared loaf or cake tin and bake in the centre of the pre-heated oven for about 25–30 minutes, checking a few minutes beforehand to see if the cake is ready: it should still be wobbly and a skewer inserted into the centre should come out almost clean. Remove from the oven and allow to rest for a few minutes before tuning out on to a wire rack to cool.

Chocolate Sponge Cake with Orange Cream Filling

This recipe is all about the filling – plenty of orange cream filling, please, and a good lacquering of chocolate topping, although this is optional. Serve with a fork and a bit of whipped cream – maybe not good for the waistline but very fulfilling! Chocolate and orange are a great match, especially in this sponge.

1. Pre-heat the oven to 170°C/325°F/Gas mark 3.

2. Cream the butter and caster sugar in a bowl until pale and creamy (an electric whisk is handy for this). While continuing to whisk, slowly add the eggs followed by the cocoa powder and ground almonds. Fold in the flour using a spatula or metal spoon and finally fold in 1 tablespoon hot water.

3. Spoon the mixture into the cake tin, level off the top and bake on the centre shelf of the pre-heated oven for about 45 minutes or until the sponge is springy to touch and just coming away from the sides of the tin. Turn out on to a wire rack and leave to cool.

4. Meanwhile, make the filling and the topping: for the filling, whisk the eggs and place in a pan with the butter, icing sugar, orange zest and juice, and lemon juice. Place over a gentle heat and stir until the mixture is thick and smooth. Pass through a sieve and allow to cool. Whip the cream and fold into the orange curd.

5. For the topping, melt the chocolate in a bowl over a pan of barely simmering water and, when melted, stir in the butter. Allow to cool a little, then add the whipped cream and mix thoroughly.

6. To serve, cut the sponge in half horizontally and spread the orange cream filling over the bottom half. Sandwich the two halves and spread the chocolate topping over the cake. Place in the fridge until required.

SERVES 8

175g (6oz) unsalted butter, softened

175g (6oz) caster sugar

3 eggs, beaten

2 tbsp cocoa powder

50g (2oz) ground almonds

175g (6oz) self-raising flour

For the orange cream filling:

2 eggs, plus 1 egg yolk

50g (2oz) butter

50g (2oz) icing sugar

zest and juice of 1 orange

juice of 1 lemon

75ml (3fl oz) double cream, whipped

For the chocolate topping (optional):

175g (6oz) plain chocolate, minimum 64% cocoa solids

25g (1oz) unsalted butter

150ml (5fl oz) double cream, whipped

1 x 20cm (8 inch) cake tin, base and sides lined with good-quality baking parchment.

Pissaladière

This is a sophisticated pizza that always proves very popular with young and old alike! Great for picnics and equally good with drinks before dinner or just left on the table for guests to help themselves to. Vary the toppings to suit yourself or the occasion, but make sure you use Homemade Tomato Sauce (see next page), which freezes well and is also a good standby with pasta or fish.

1. Place the flour, sea salt flakes and softened butter into the bowl of a food mixer.

2. Using the dough hook or 'K' beater, mix thoroughly. Combine the yeast and sugar in a bowl. Mix with your fingertips so that the yeast breaks down and becomes smooth and almost liquid. Add the milk and beaten egg and then mix thoroughly.

3. With the machine still running, slowly add the yeast mixture to the flour, then allow the machine to knead the dough for 5–8 minutes, or until it comes away from the sides of the bowl and does not stick to your hands. Remove the bowl from the mixer and cover the dough with a clean, damp tea towel. Place in the fridge and leave for about 2 hours.

4. Turn the dough out on to a lightly floured work surface. Knead well with the palm of your hand, then roll out into a rectangular shape about 30 x 25cm (12 x 10 inches). Place the dough on a non-stick baking tray of similar proportions. Press the dough into the corners, then spread the tomato sauce over the top.

MAKES 1 LARGE
PISSALADIÈRE (SERVES 8)

275g (10oz) strong plain flour

good pinch of Maldon sea salt flakes

75g (3oz) softened salted butter

generous 15g (½oz) fresh yeast

1 tsp caster sugar

150ml (5fl oz) lukewarm milk

1 egg, beaten

For the topping:

1 quantity Homemade Tomato Sauce (see next page)

about 8 thin slices Parma ham

2 pieces buffalo mozzarella, broken up into thumb-sized pieces

75g (3oz) mixed black and green olives, pitted

small can anchovy fillets, drained and sliced lengthways

2 tbsp small capers, rinsed and drained

fresh basil or tarragon leaves

olive oil

freshly ground black pepper

Maldon sea salt flakes

5. Next, loosely place the slices of Parma ham over the tomato sauce then scatter over the mozzarella, olives, anchovies and capers. Add a good grinding of black pepper, then scatter the torn basil or tarragon leaves all over the top.

6. Place somewhere warm and leave for an hour until risen and doubled in size.

7. Pre-heat the oven to 200°C/400°F/Gas mark 6.

8. When the dough has risen, drizzle over a little olive oil and bake in the pre-heated oven for 20–25 minutes until the crust is golden and crisp. Remove from the oven, scatter over a few flakes of sea salt and serve warm, cut into squares.

12 medium, ripe vine-grown tomatoes, quartered

55ml (2fl oz) sunflower oil

2 shallots, finely chopped

1 garlic clove, grated

1 fresh thyme sprig

1 tbsp malt vinegar

pinch of sugar

seasoning

Homemade Tomato Sauce

1. Pre-heat the oven to 140°C/275°F/Gas mark 1.

2. Mix all the ingredients together, then spread them evenly over a large baking sheet. Place in the pre-heated oven and cook for about 1½ hours, by which time the moisture will have evaporated and the tomatoes will have started to dry out a little.

3. Remove from the oven and blitz in a liquidiser before passing through a fine sieve into a bowl.

Summer eating is synonymous with picnics – weather permitting of course – be it fighting to keep the sand out of the sandwiches on a windy beach as the windbreak struggles to stay upright, or spreading a rug on the grass by a river to doze the afternoon away in a surfeit of potted meats and pickles. The choice of food is critical: the keyword is portable, with foods that stay the course rather than collapsing or wilting in the heat. Picnic foods need to be robust, easy to carry and easy to eat – which is why traditional favourites such as pork pie, Scotch eggs and chicken salads have long been standard fare.

Childhood picnics were a mainstay of my summer holidays on the north Norfolk coast. Once, my father even cooked boiled leg of mutton in a large pot, covered with veg, when we were staying at the Watch House near Blakeney, which had no mod cons. We had to gather driftwood for the fire to cook on, and dig a pit for the loo! There was a larder at the Watch House so we could keep some foods fresh for a while. My mother used to bring a jelly mould of junket with her from our home in Hainford, about forty minutes' drive away. Of course we also ate endless sweets. Another holiday favourite was poached strawberries, as the poaching meant they kept for longer.

For picnics on the beach, again the food would be brought from Hainford. A family favourite was a raised pie and my mother brought a box of eggs covered in jelly! We also used to eat lots of corn on the cob, slathered in butter.

Nowadays our picnics are classier. We usually go out with crab and lobster, which the boys love – in fact, it's Harry's favourite food, along with shell-on prawns. We put our boat, Funny Tern, in the water from Easter onwards and try to find time to go fishing for mackerel using brightly coloured feathers in six lines off a hook. Then we cook our catch on the boat, washed down with copious quantities of white wine!

The sea is a huge part of both our work and home lives. Tides and weather permitting, we'd rather go out on the boat than do anything else, so most of our days out are spent on the water. We take some wine, a picnic and a pint of prawns – heaven! We're not far from home but it feels like a million miles away and when the weather's right you could be anywhere in the world. And when we're not on the boat we go crabbing, cockling and shrimping which provides ready-made picnics of the freshest type.

Scotch Quails' Eggs

Perfect for picnics, this traditional favourite is given a modern twist here and, while it's true that your own homemade Scotch eggs may require a little effort, they are a million miles away from anything you can buy. Using quails' eggs also makes them more child-friendly and more likely to go in the mouth than fall on the ground! I would suggest you make at least a dozen of these Scotch eggs. The recipe may seem a little complicated but actually it is not – and these will probably be the best Scotch eggs you have tasted! They will keep for several days in the fridge.

MAKES 12 SCOTCH EGGS

12 quails' eggs

350g (12oz) pork sausagemeat

2 tbsp chopped fresh tarragon

1 medium egg yolk, beaten

seasoned plain flour, for coating

1 egg and 4 tbsp milk, whisked together

75g (3oz) Panko Japanese breadcrumbs, or stale bread, left out overnight so it blitzes well for breadcrumbs

570ml (1 pint) sunflower oil, for shallow frying

seasoning

1. Bring a pan of salted water to the boil. Lower in the quails' eggs and boil for 3 minutes. Remove from the boiling water and plunge immediately into cold, running water. When cold, peel carefully and set aside in a bowl of cold water.

2. In a bowl, combine the sausagemeat, tarragon and beaten egg yolk. Season with salt and pepper, mix well and divide into 12 portions.

3. Have ready three plates: on the first one, spread out some seasoned flour, put the egg wash on to the second plate and on the third plate spread out the breadcrumbs. Drain the quails' eggs and dry them on a towel. Take one portion of sausagemeat and flatten it out in the palm of your hand, place a quail's egg into the centre of the sausagemeat then wrap the meat around the egg so that it is totally encased. Roll it into a little ball and repeat with the other eggs.

4. Roll each Scotch egg in seasoned flour, then dip into the egg wash, shaking off any excess. Finally, roll in breadcrumbs to coat thoroughly and place on to a baking sheet covered with greaseproof paper.

5. Pour enough oil into a medium-sized, heavy-based pan to come no more than one-third of the way up the side. Heat the oil to approximately 160°C/320°F (use a thermometer, or test the temperature by dropping in a small nugget of sausagemeat; if it rises immediately to the top and starts to fry, the oil is at the correct temperature).

6. Carefully lower the Scotch eggs into the hot oil and fry until well-coloured all over. You may need to do this in batches; if so, make sure the oil comes back up to temperature before frying the next batch.

7. Remove the cooked eggs with a slotted spoon and drain on kitchen paper.

A Perfect Picnic
Pork Pie with Piccalilli

1. Begin by making the stock. Place the pigs' trotters in a heavy-based pan, cover with cold water, bring to the boil and simmer for 10 minutes, skimming off any scum that rises to the surface. Drain the trotters, rinse thoroughly in cold, running water and return to the cleaned-out pan with the remaining stock ingredients. Add enough cold water to just cover, bring to the boil and simmer very slowly for 2 hours. Strain the stock into another pan, bring back to the boil and reduce until you have 275ml (10fl oz) liquid. Set aside to cool.

2. Next, make the pastry. Place the flour and salt into a bowl. In a pan, bring the lard and 200ml (7fl oz) water to the boil, then pour this over the flour and mix well. Turn out on to a lightly floured work surface and gather together. Leave to rest out of the fridge for 30 minutes.

3. Mix all the filling ingredients together in a bowl. Season well with salt and pepper.

4. Pre-heat the oven to 200°C/400°F/Gas mark 6.

5. To assemble and cook the pie: take two-thirds of the pastry and roll it out on a lightly floured work surface in a circle larger than the base of the flan ring. Line the base and the sides of the flan ring, using your fingers to push the pastry up and just over the sides. You do not want the pastry to be too thin.

6. Spoon the filling into the lined flan ring and press down firmly. Brush round the top edge of the pastry with beaten egg.

7. Roll out the remaining pastry into a circle the same size as the flan ring, place it over the top of the flan ring and crimp around the two edges of the pastry to seal, using a little more of the beaten egg if necessary. Make a small hole in the centre of the pastry lid.

8. Place the pie in the centre of the pre-heated oven for 40 minutes, then turn the temperature down to 170°C/325°F/Gas mark 3 and cook for a further 45 minutes, until the pastry is well coloured. Remove from the oven and set aside to cool.

9. When cool, pour the cooled (but not set) stock into the pie through the hole in the centre of the pastry. Place in the fridge overnight to set.

SERVES 6-8

For the stock:

2 pigs' trotters, split lengthways (your butcher will do this for you)

1 carrot

1 onion, peeled and chopped

1 stick celery

glass of white wine

For the pastry:

350g (12oz) self-raising flour

1 tsp salt

110g (4oz) lard

1 egg, beaten (for sealing the pastry)

For the filling:

450g (1lb) shoulder of pork, cut into 2.5 cm (1 inch) cubes

250g (9oz) pork belly, minced

275g (10oz) sausagemeat

110g (4oz) smoked back bacon, chopped

1 Cox's apple, peeled, cored and diced

2 large field mushrooms, chopped

1 tbsp chopped fresh sage

seasoning

1 x 20cm (8 inch) loose-bottomed flan ring.

Piccalilli

1. Begin by making up the pickling vinegar. Place all the ingredients in a pan, over a low heat, until the sugar has dissolved. Bring to the boil and simmer gently for a couple of minutes. Leave to cool, then strain into a jug and set aside.

2. Meanwhile, trim and dice all the vegetables into small cubes (the onions can either be left whole, halved or quartered, depending on their size). Pour 2 litres (3½ pints) water into a large bowl and stir in the salt. Place all the vegetables into the salted water and leave to soak overnight.

3. The next morning, drain and wash the vegetables in plenty of cold, running water and place in a large bowl.

4. Using another bowl, mix the finely chopped chilli, cornflour, turmeric and Dijon mustard to a runny paste with about 150ml (5fl oz) of the cold, strained pickling vinegar. Bring the remainder of the vinegar back to the boil in a clean pan over a moderate heat, stir in the paste mixture and cook for 2-3 minutes, stirring continuously, until it thickens.

5. Pour the hot mixture over the vegetables and mix thoroughly. Fill five jam jars, each 450g (1lb) capacity, with the piccalilli and when really cool, cover and seal.

MAKES 5 JARS, EACH 450G (1LB)

For the pickling vinegar:
570ml (1 pint) white wine vinegar
15g (½oz) fresh red chilli, diced
250g (9oz) caster sugar
50g (2oz) grated horseradish (or horseradish sauce)
2-3 fresh thyme sprigs
1 bay leaf

For the piccalilli:
300g (10½oz) red peppers
200g (7oz) yellow peppers
200g (7oz) cucumber, peeled
200g (7oz) courgettes
200g (7oz) button or pickling onions
200g (7oz) fennel
200g (7oz) celery
florets from 1 small cauliflower
40g (1½oz) salt

To finish:
1 large fresh red chilli approx 40g (1½oz), finely chopped
40g (1½oz) cornflour
15g (½oz) ground turmeric
75g (3oz) Dijon mustard

Couscous and Quinoa Salad with Mediterranean Vegetables

SERVES 6

110g (4oz) quinoa

110g (4oz) couscous

150ml (5fl oz) boiling water

olive oil

1 red onion, peeled and chopped

3 garlic cloves, peeled and grated with a microplane grater

1 medium aubergine, fairly finely diced

1 large courgette, fairly finely diced

1 each red, yellow and orange peppers, diced

1 small fennel bulb, finely chopped

juice of 1 lemon

large bunch of fresh basil, chopped

seasoning

I had tended to steer clear of couscous and quinoa for many years because their origins were not local and I really didn't know much about them. But they're ideal ingredients for a picnic, and this salad is colourful, fresh, light, summery, very healthy and easy to transport. Quinoa makes an interesting contrast to other salad ingredients: packed with flavour and nutritional value, it's a good vegetarian choice too.

1. To cook the quinoa, follow the instructions on the pack, then leave to cool. Place the couscous in a large bowl and pour over the boiling water. Mix well, cover with clingfilm and leave to cool while you prepare and cook the vegetables.

2. Heat a large, heavy-based frying pan, add 2 tablespoons olive oil and fry the onion and garlic until soft but not coloured. Next, add the aubergine, courgette, peppers and fennel, adding a little more olive oil if necessary and continue to cook until the vegetables have softened a little. Remove from the heat, season well and allow to cool.

3. Remove the clingfilm from the couscous and gently stir through with a fork to separate the grains. Mix in the quinoa then stir in the lemon juice and 3 tablespoons olive oil, followed by the cooled vegetables. Season to taste and, just before serving, stir in plenty of chopped basil.

Lightly Curried Chicken Breasts with Mango Mayonnaise

SERVES 6

6 free-range chicken breasts, skin left on

1 large shallot, roughly chopped

1 garlic clove, peeled

2.5cm (1 inch) piece of fresh root ginger

2 lemon grass stalks

juice of 1 lemon

½ tsp ground turmeric

½ tsp garam masala

275ml (10fl oz) coconut milk

1 tbsp full-fat yoghurt

2 large red chillies, seeded and finely chopped

bunch of fresh coriander, chopped

seasoning

If your 'picnic' is at home, then roast these in the oven or cook them on the barbecue and eat them hot. Alternatively, cook them in advance and eat cold. Either way, they are great, especially when accompanied by Mango Mayonnaise (see recipe below).

1. Cut each chicken breast lengthways into three and place in a large bowl.

2. Place the remaining ingredients in a liquidiser and blitz thoroughly (you may need to stop the machine and push the contents down to ensure everything gets thoroughly liquidised). Taste and season.

3. Pour the coconut milk mixture over the chicken breast strips and mix carefully. Cover with clingfilm and place in the fridge to marinate for as long as possible, preferably overnight.

4. Pre-heat the oven to 190°C/375°F/Gas mark 5.

5. When you are ready to cook the chicken, place it in a roasting tin and cook in the pre-heated oven for about 15 minutes, turning the strips fairly frequently to ensure they are cooked right through. Serve hot or cold with Mango Mayonnaise.

1 egg

1 tsp white wine vinegar

½ tsp Dijon mustard

275ml (½ pint) sunflower oil

zest and juice of ½ lime

1 ripe mango

seasoning

Mango Mayonnaise

This mayonnaise has real zing and a wonderful mango flavour.

1. Place the egg, vinegar and Dijon mustard in the bowl of a food processor, season with salt and pepper and whiz well. With the machine still running, slowly add the sunflower oil in a steady stream until the mixture has emulsified and thickened. Once you have added all the oil, pour in the lime juice and add the zest.

2. Scrape the mayonnaise out of the food processor into a bowl.

3. Peel the mango and place the flesh in the bowl of the processor. Whiz to a purée then fold this into the mayonnaise and check the seasoning.

Kipper Pâté

I know this is a bit of blast from the past, but homemade kipper pâté is delicious. Now that we have our own smoker at Morston, we make this by cold-smoking wonderful fresh local herrings. If you don't have your own smoker, good-quality kippers will work just as well; or buy 500g/1lb 2oz cooked kipper fillets (if using these, there's no need to grill them). Be prepared to add a little extra cream to achieve the right consistency. A relaxed attitude and flexibility are the key words here – trust me, the flavour will be delicious! Serve with hot buttered toast.

SERVES 6

6 decent-sized kippers, about 250g/9oz each with the head on
a little butter
200g (7oz) full-fat cream cheese
juice of ½ lemon
1 tsp horseradish
pinch of paprika
1 tbsp snipped chives
1 tbsp double cream
good grinding of black pepper

1. Pre-heat the grill.

2. Lay the butterflied (opened out) kippers on a grill tray and spread a little butter over them. Grill gently until the flesh starts to come away from the bones, then remove and allow to cool a little.

3. Carefully pick over the fish, removing all the bones (you should end up with about 500g/1lb 2oz kipper flesh). Place the fish in the bowl of a food processor with the cream cheese, lemon juice, horseradish, paprika and a good grinding of black pepper. Pulse the food processor until you have a coarse soft pâté. Finally, pulse in the snipped chives and double cream.

4. Place in a suitable container, cover with clingfilm and store in the fridge until needed.

KIPPERS

We went to have lunch with one of our wine suppliers – Blaise Le Mesurier (as in the late John, of *Dad's Army* fame) – and ate in the garden where there was a wooden temple-like structure with a fish on the outside. Thinking he was into some wacky religion, I soon discovered that it was, in fact, a smokehouse he'd built himself. He then produced the most amazing tray of prawns, which he'd smoked. We ate them with mayonnaise, then smoked salmon. So we sat outside, enjoying lunch and getting rather drunk!

I got my builder to copy it and we have used it for kippers, wild garlic, haddock, duck legs and (less successfully) tomatoes (which just tasted burnt). It cold smokes, so everything has to be brined. We smoke over hand-sawn oak shavings which give a less harsh result than machine-sawn shavings. It's shown me that freshness is paramount: we get our herrings from Lowestoft and they're brimmingly fresh so as a result the kippers – and this pàté – are fabulous.

Smoked Salmon and Brown Shrimp Roll

At Morston, we make a lot of smoked salmon and we will always use the saltier, thinner tail end, as it's a good way of using it up. Equally good is to make the mousse, fold in the shrimps and serve with brown toast or serve as a canapé topping. Warm asparagus, a poached egg and maybe some lightly dressed leaves make a good accompaniment to this lovely light summer dish.

1. Begin by making the mousse: blitz the smoked salmon and lime juice in a food processor until smooth. In the kitchen at Morston we would then pass this through a sieve or tamis into a bowl, but at home you could just scrape the mousse into a large bowl if you prefer.

2. Next, slowly add the cream a little at a time, beating really well with a spatula between each addition until you achieve a 'dropping' consistency (you may not need to use all the cream). Fold in the chives, shrimps and a good grinding of black pepper, then cover with clingfilm and set aside.

3. Lay 2 sheets of clingfilm, about 35 x 35cm (14 x 14 inches), on top of each other on a work surface and cover this with the thin slices of smoked salmon. Using a potato peeler, peel the cucumber lengthways into very thin, long, wide strips, discarding the seeds when you reach them.

4. Place the thin strips of cucumber over the smoked salmon and then spread the salmon mousse over the cucumber, leaving a 2.5cm (1 inch) border to avoid excess spillage of the mixture when rolling it up. Roll it up very tightly in the clingfilm like a sausage, tie each end and place in the fridge (the roll can be made up to three days before serving).

5. When ready to serve, use a sharp, serrated knife to slice the roll (still with the clingfilm around it) and remove the clingfilm as you place the slices on to plates.

SERVES 6 VERY GENEROUSLY

275g (10oz) smoked salmon, ideally from the tail end, skinned and chopped, plus about 275g (10oz) extra smoked salmon, thinly sliced

juice of 1 lime

200ml (7fl oz) double cream

3 tbsp finely snipped chives

175g (6oz) peeled brown shrimps

good grinding of black pepper

1 cucumber, peeled

Summer Garden Salad with Raspberry Vinaigrette

This salad includes everything that's so great about summer eating – I don't reckon you could really want for anything more. It also makes the most of seasonal radishes and beetroot, of which I'm a massive fan. Bright and colourful, everything in this bowl smacks of summer, and the raspberry vinaigrette adds a really fruity hit and slight sweetness.

1. Prepare all the ingredients and combine them in a large bowl. When you are ready to serve, season with salt and pepper and dress lightly with Raspberry Vinaigrette (see opposite).

SERVES 6

3 Little Gem lettuces, outer leaves removed, picked over, washed and patted dry

12 really ripe small vine tomatoes, quartered

12 radishes, washed and quartered

½ cucumber, chopped into chunks

handful of garden peas, shelled but not cooked

12 small, freshly dug new potatoes, scraped and boiled in salted water with fresh mint

handful of broad beans, shelled and very briefly cooked in salted water (about 30 seconds) so that you can slip the skins off easily

2 beetroot, cooked and chopped

3 medium eggs, lightly hard-boiled

75g (3oz) English blue vein cheese (this could be Stilton or Binham Blue), broken into bite-sized pieces

12 small spring onions, washed

lots of chopped herbs, such as tarragon, chives, mint and parsley

2 tbsp chopped blanched hazelnuts

1 avocado, peeled and chopped

1 small mango, peeled and cut into chunks

1 small can salted anchovies, thinly sliced lengthways (optional)

seasoning

For the raspberry vinegar:
450g (1lb) really ripe raspberries
225ml (8fl oz) white vine vinegar
150g (5oz) caster sugar
120ml (4fl oz) boiling water
pinch of salt

For the raspberry vinaigrette:
8 tbsp raspberry vinegar
1 tsp Dijon mustard
8 tbsp olive oil
juice of 1 lime
seasoning

Raspberry Vinaigrette

This is one of my favourite dressings. It's worth making quite a large quantity of the vinaigrette (as here), because it does keep in the fridge in a clean screw-top jar for three to four weeks, as does the intensely flavoured raspberry vinegar.

1. First, make the raspberry vinegar. In a bowl, soak half the raspberries in the vinegar and sugar. Pour over the boiling water, add the salt, cover with clingfilm and set aside overnight.

2. The next day, pour the mixture into a sieve over a bowl and leave to drip through without pressing the raspberries. Add the second half of the raspberries to the sieved vinegar and sit the bowl over a pan of barely simmering water for about 1 hour. Strain again, allow to cool and store in the fridge in a clean, screw-top jar.

3. To make the vinaigrette, place the raspberry vinegar in a bowl, whisk in the Dijon mustard, olive oil and lime juice, then season to taste. Keep in a screw-top jar and shake well before using.

Smoked Haddock and Watercress Tart

Most people associate watercress with a salad. Delicious, yes, but summery haddock and watercress go really well together due to the peppery nature of the watercress. The addition of water chestnuts adds a lovely crunchiness.

1. Pre-heat the oven to 180°C/350°F/Gas mark 4.

2. Cover the pastry-lined flan ring with baking parchment, fill with baking beans and place in the centre of the pre-heated oven. Bake 'blind' for about 20 minutes, or until the pastry just starts to colour.

3. Carefully remove the baking beans and parchment. Brush the sides and base of the pastry case with egg wash to ensure that any cracks get sealed and return to the oven for a further 5 minutes. Leave to cool.

4. Next, blanch the watercress: bring a pan of salted water to the boil, drop in the watercress and boil for 30 seconds only. Refresh under cold, running water, drain well, dry in a tea towel and set aside.

5. Lay the haddock on a board and cut into 2.5cm (1 inch) cubes.

6. In a bowl, combine the eggs, egg yolks and double cream with a good grating of nutmeg and mix well. Add the haddock, water chestnuts and a light seasoning of salt and pepper and mix well again.

7. Place the cooked pastry case on a baking sheet and spread the watercress over the base. Carefully ladle in the smoked haddock and water chestnut custard and place in the centre of the pre-heated oven.

8. Bake for 20 minutes, sprinkle over the Gruyère cheese and bake for a further 20 minutes or until the custard has almost set (it should still be very slightly wobbly in the centre). Remove from the oven and leave to cool.

SERVES 6

20cm (8 inch) removable base flan tin, lined with savoury shortcrust pastry

1 egg, beaten, for egg wash

For the filling:

125g (4½oz) watercress

1 fillet of undyed smoked haddock, about 450g (1lb), skinned and bones removed

3 eggs, plus 2 egg yolks

225ml (8fl oz) double cream

good grating of fresh nutmeg

1 small can water chestnuts, drained well and diced into chunks

75g (3oz) grated Gruyère cheese

seasoning

Sticky Banana Tea Bread

Tea breads and malt loaves are always so moreish that once the loaf is sliced and spread with butter it's impossible not to keep on going back to it until the whole loaf is eaten! This one is no exception. It also tastes even better after a couple of days and is good for a picnic as it slices beautifully.

MAKES ENOUGH FOR A 900G (2LB) LOAF TIN

150g (5oz) sultanas

125g (4 1/2 oz) raisins

125g (4 1/2 oz) currants

50g (2oz) glacé cherries, rinsed, dried and chopped into chunks

275ml (1/2 pint) leftover cold tea (if you add an extra teabag then so much the better)

2 bananas, mashed up with a fork

200g (7oz) demerara sugar

100g (3 1/2 oz) pecan nuts, chopped

1 egg, beaten with 2 tbsp milk and 2 tbsp black treacle

400g (14oz) self-raising flour

1 x 900g (2lb) loaf tin, lined with good-quality, silicone-coated greaseproof paper.

1. The night before baking the bread, place all the fruits except for the bananas in a bowl, pour over the tea and leave overnight to marinate.

2. Pre-heat the oven to 170°C/325°F/Gas mark 3.

3. The next day, add all the remaining ingredients and beat in well. Pour the mixture into the prepared loaf tin and bake in the pre-heated oven for 1 hour 15 minutes until a skewer inserted into the centre comes out almost dry (there may still be a little stickiness).

4. Remove from the oven and turn out on to a wire rack to cool.

SUM
DIN
PART

MER
NER
IES

Thankfully, things have moved on from the days when the beleaguered hostess would spend three days in the kitchen preparing a succession of dishes with which to wow her dinner guests. These days, entertaining is more relaxed – and relaxing – and, at home, I prefer to adopt a more casual approach too.

We rarely have formal dinner parties – if we're not working, we're running around with the children – and hardly ever use our dining room. So if we do entertain it's mostly spur-of-the-moment kitchen suppers as I much prefer taking the dish to the table. Keep it simple and relaxed is my mantra, so most dishes I cook for friends – and those in this chapter – can be prepared in advance.

Like us, more people are having kitchen suppers now rather than old-fashioned formal dinner parties, but there are certain occasions when something more formal is what you want. You can, of course, have a summer dinner party outside or in the kitchen, but whatever you do, the key to successful entertaining is to prepare everything well in advance so you have as little last-minute hassle as possible. I hope that message runs throughout the book.

Another important element of summer entertaining is eating an ingredient when it's in season and at its best – it hasn't been forced, so freshness and flavour are as good as they can be. Seasonal foods should also be cheaper and won't have clocked up the air miles. I have no interest in looking further than my backyard! You can get so many things locally – we even have sweetcorn, which needs to be eaten as soon as possible after picking. Anything that's freshly picked has to be massively better than something that's been sitting around wilting or in a shop for days.

Lobster and crabs are some of my favourite summer foods but don't have to be complicated. Grilled lobster with salad is perfect and although it is expensive, you can use the shells to make a fantastic bisque or stock. The same goes for crab – most of the flavour is in the shells.

Peas are good here too. My friend Neil Alston used to farm peas which then went to a large frozen pea processing company. He'd bring me ones that had been caught in the machine, so weren't suitable for processing. I do think frozen peas are fine to use, but in summer, if you can get the real thing, do. Neil's peas were the real petits pois variety – really sweet, but like all pulses they have to be eaten fresh for their full impact and flavour. Broad beans and carrots are the same.

Sea Trout, Leek and Potato Terrine with Tomato Butter Sauce

This terrine looks stunning – sea trout, watercress and new potatoes make for a great visual combination, as well as tasting terrific – and has to be prepared in advance, which is ideal for hassle-free entertaining. Although I have given a weight of sea trout, you actually need two reasonably thick pieces that will fit snugly into a 28cm x 11cm and 8cm deep (11 x 4 x 3 inch) terrine mould. You can cook the sea trout and potatoes in olive oil instead of duck fat if you prefer, but duck fat gives a lovely flavour and keeps the fish very moist. It is easier to handle sea trout if you leave the skin on till after it is cooked. You could also serve this with Beurre Blanc (see next page). I like to use wild or organic fish where possible simply because the flesh has a better texture and the flavour is deeper. Sea trout are in season from May to September and are caught along the sandy stretches of the coast.

1. Line the terrine mould with a double layer of clingfilm, leaving plenty of overhang so you can cover the top later: the easiest way to do this is to oil the terrine very lightly with a little vegetable oil, then push the double layer of clingfilm well into the corners using a tea towel.

2. Cut the sea trout in half lengthways, using the terrine mould as a guide for width and length (the sea trout will eventually make two layers in the terrine).

3. Melt the duck fat in a high-sided roasting tin large enough to hold the sea trout pieces. Heat it to 53–55°C (130°F) then carefully slide in the sea trout pieces. At the same temperature, cook the sea trout for 25–30 minutes until just cooked but still pink and moist. Remove the sea trout from the fat in whole pieces and set aside, leaving the fat in the tin.

4. While the sea trout is cooking, remove the outer leaves from the leeks until you have enough to line the terrine. Finely slice the remaining green of the leek, discarding the white part. Blanch the whole outer leaves in boiling, salted water for 2 minutes. Drain and refresh in cold water, then drain again thoroughly and pat dry in a clean tea towel.

SERVES 10

1–2 kg (2lb 4oz–4lb 8oz) wild or organic sea trout, pinboned but skin left on

enough duck fat (or olive oil) to cover the sea trout

2 leeks

110g (4oz) unsalted butter

200g (7oz) watercress, chopped

10 medium English new potatoes

seasoning

5. Heat the butter in a pan, add the sliced leeks and cook gently until soft. Add the chopped watercress, season and cook until wilted. Set aside.

6. Bring the fat back up to about 90°C (195°F). Peel the potatoes and cut into 7mm (¼ inch) slices. Carefully slide the sliced potatoes into the fat and cook for about 15 minutes, until very soft. Using a slotted spoon, remove to a wire rack to drain.

7. Line the terrine with the whole, blanched leek leaves, overlapping them and allowing a good overhang. Spread half of the leek and watercress mixture over the bottom of the terrine, then season. Remove the skin from the sea trout, then place one piece on top of the leeks. Season, then add half the potato slices and season again. Repeat this process with the remaining ingredients, seasoning each layer as you do so.

8. Fold the overhanging leek leaves over the terrine and then fold the clingfilm over this, sides first, then the ends. Pierce the clingfilm around the edge of the terrine to release the juices when pressing.

9. Place a board, which just fits inside the mould, on top of the terrine and then place a weight on top of that. Place on a tray and chill overnight.

10. To serve, unmould the terrine. Cut a thin slice off the end through the clingfilm and discard. Slice the terrine through the clingfilm, remembering to remove the clingfilm afterwards. Serve with the Tomato Butter Sauce and Beurre Blanc (see next page).

SERVES 10

450g (1lb) vine-ripened tomatoes

75g (3oz) unsalted butter

1 tsp caster sugar

seasoning

SERVES 10

2 shallots, peeled and finely sliced

1 tbsp wine vinegar

2 tbsp lemon juice

4 tbsp white wine

225g (8oz) salted butter, cut into cubes

Tomato Butter Sauce

1. Quarter half the tomatoes, remove the seeds and place them in a liquidiser. Add the remaining tomatoes, quartered but seeds left in. Blend thoroughly. Push the puréed tomatoes through a fine sieve.

2. To serve, warm the tomatoes in a pan over a low heat, whisk in the butter, add the sugar, and season to taste.

Butter Sauce (Beurre Blanc)

1. Place the shallots, wine vinegar, lemon juice and white wine in a pan. Bring to the boil and reduce the liquid until you have about 1 tablespoon. Add 1 tablespoon cold water and reduce again until you have 1 tablespoon liquid.

2. Turn the heat down and, over a low heat, slowly whisk in the butter, about 25g (1oz) at a time. The sauce will emulsify (thicken and lighten in colour). Once all the butter has been added, remove the pan from the heat, and then pass the sauce through a sieve into another pan. Set aside until needed, but do not chill or the sauce will separate.

3. To serve, gently reheat the sauce, stirring continuously.

Grilled Lobster with Garlic and Lime Butter

SERVES 6

For a main course allow 1 lobster per person, each weighing no more than 750g (1lb 10oz)

For the garlic and lime butter:

125g (4½oz) salted butter, softened

2 garlic cloves, peeled and crushed into a purée

1 tbsp chopped fresh coriander

zest and juice of 1 lime

freshly ground black pepper

This is my favourite summer dinner party dish as it relies on brimmingly fresh ingredients simply prepared, which is always my watchword for the very best food. Lobster still has a ring of decadence to it, so this is a luxurious treat to serve your guests. Serve with freshly dug, scraped new potatoes boiled with a handful of mint and some lightly boiled samphire if you can get it.

1. Mix the garlic and lime butter ingredients together and keep at room temperature until required.

2. Pre-heat the grill to hot.

3. Unless the lobsters are ready-cooked, plunge them into rapidly boiling, salted water for no more than 5 minutes. Crack the claws and remove the claw meat, trying to keep it as whole as possible.

4. Split the lobsters in half from head to tail and lay them, shell side down, on to a grill tray. Sit the claw meat on top of the lobster's head.

5. Generously spread the garlic and lime butter over the lobster flesh and flash them under the pre-heated grill for 2 minutes until everything is bubbling.

6. Serve immediately.

LOBSTER

If you could give me lobster every day, I'd be happy! Lobster and crabs are the best ingredients but don't have to be complicated. Grilled lobster with salad is my desert island dish. A huge number of lobsters are caught along our coast from Mundesley to Brancaster with each village claiming their lobster as the best, but the sad thing is that most end up being exported as people here think of them as an extremely expensive food, or don't want to have to prepare them. They aren't cheap but you can get two meals out of them if you use the shells for a lovely lobster bisque or to make some stock.

Eating a food in season means you're eating it at its most flavourful and freshest and with lobster this means a real treat! As well as simply grilled, it's a great food to barbecue as it's quite meaty in texture. If we have friends round we always aim to eat outside and my ideal meal would be half a lobster, shell-on prawns, crab and salad and some good bread – something that involves little work, but relies on really good, fresh ingredients. When buying lobster choose one that feels heavy as it will have more meat.

As with the rest of our seafood, we get our lobsters from Willie Weston at Blakeney. When I first met him he was operating out of a little house behind Blakeney surgery, working as a lugworm digger who occasionally got a few lobsters and crabs. Nowadays he brings in several container loads a week and sends them off to Spain. With our suppliers, I do realise that we're living in a bit of a bubble up here as we're really lucky to have so many wonderful foods on our doorstep and don't have to rely on supermarkets for shopping. It's great that we can go to the fishmonger, the butcher and build up a working relationship with them. There's so much play nowadays on regional and seasonal food, but it's something I've been doing for years!

Roast Double Loin of Lamb with Roasted Shallot Purée

Double loin of lamb is not an unusual cut and is easy to prepare. Your butcher will know what you mean by it; if buying the meat from a supermarket you could try asking them to order some in for you. Make sure the fillets are still intact underneath and the flanks have been trimmed off. You could serve this with Norfolk-style New Potatoes with Bacon, Samphire and Soya Beans (page 146).

1. Pre-heat the oven to 200°C/400°F/Gas mark 6.

2. Heat a large frying pan till very hot. Add a good splash of olive oil, then place one of the loins in the hot pan, skin side down. Seal, turning now and then, until the skin is really blistered and well coloured. Season as you do so, then repeat with the other loin.

3. Place the chopped vegetables, garlic and herbs in a roasting tin, then sit the loins on top, skin side uppermost.

4. Roast in the oven for 25–30 minutes. Remove and set aside somewhere warm to rest for a few minutes.

5. Carve in the conventional way, or lengthways along the bone, which is much easier than it might appear. Scatter with any intact garlic cloves and serve with Roasted Shallot Purée.

Roasted Shallot Purée

1. Pre-heat the oven to 180°C/350°F/Gas mark 4.

2. Lay two large sheets of foil on top of each other on a work surface. Place the shallots in the centre of the foil, pour over the olive oil, add the thyme and season well. Draw the sides of the foil up to the centre and crinkle the edges to seal and form a parcel. Place on a baking sheet and bake in the oven for about 1½ hours, until the shallots are really soft.

3. Remove the papery skin from the shallots and place in a liquidiser with the butter and cream. Blitz really well and pour into a bowl. Check the seasoning. To serve, gently re-heat when needed.

SERVES 6

2 double loins of lamb, each about 18cm (7 inches) in length and weighing about 900g–1.15kg (2–2½lb)

oil, for frying

1 medium onion, chopped

2 carrots, chopped

1 celery stick, chopped

at least 12 garlic cloves

1 fresh rosemary sprig

1 bunch of fresh mint

seasoning

900g (2lb) shallots, ends just trimmed

120ml (4fl oz) olive oil

1 fresh thyme sprig

knob of butter

6 tbsp double cream

seasoning

Sea Trout en Papillote

Sea trout is seasonal and the best time to catch it is between May and September, although we have noticed locally that it's available beyond its usual season nowadays – maybe the consequence of global warming. If getting hold of it is a problem, use fresh salmon instead. Serve with boiled new potatoes and buttery samphire. You can prepare the parcels in advance of cooking.

1. Lay out on your work surface 6 pieces of greaseproof paper about 35cm (14 inches) square.

2. Using a sharp knife, slice the sea trout fillets into short strips about 2.5cm (1 inch) wide and place 5 or 6 strips into the centre of each piece of greaseproof paper.

3. Add a chunk of lemon grass, a tablespoon each of petits pois, white wine and olive oil. Season with salt and pepper and scatter over some chopped dill.

4. Now carefully fold over one corner of the greaseproof paper to the other to make triangular parcel. Next, fold each of the two open sides tightly over, to seal the parcel.

5. Pre-heat the oven to 180°C/350°F/Gas mark 6.

6. Place the parcels on a large baking sheet, sprinkle over a little cold water and cook in the pre-heated oven for 5–6 minutes. Serve immediately, allowing each person to open their own parcel at the table.

SERVES 6

1 sea trout, weighing approximately 1kg (2lb 4oz), skinned, filleted and pinboned

2 sticks of lemon grass, bruised with the back of a knife and each cut into 3 chunks

6 tbsp frozen or fresh petits pois

6 tbsp white wine

6 tbsp olive oil

handful of chopped fresh dill

seasoning

Fresh Garden Pea and Mint Soup

White crab meat or really crisp grilled streaky bacon make excellent accompaniments to this soup. You can serve this warm or chilled – although, apart from gazpacho, I personally prefer to have a soup hot or warm, even in the summer. I have specified English onions as they have a stronger flavour, and why go to Spain for them if you can get them closer to home? Peas are another favourite summer food of mine … nothing beats the sweetness of a freshly picked pea; if you can't find these, the next best thing is to use frozen.

SERVES 6

25g (1oz) butter

2 medium English onions, peeled and sliced

1 garlic clove, peeled and sliced

good pinch of sugar

570g (1lb 4oz) shelled garden peas or frozen petits pois

handful of fresh mint leaves

4 tbsp double cream

seasoning

1. Melt the butter in a large pan; add the onions and garlic and cook to soften without colouring, then set aside.

2. Bring 450ml (16fl oz) water to the boil in a pan. Add salt and a good pinch of sugar, throw in the petits pois and cook until just tender.

3. Remove from the heat, add the mint leaves and immediately blitz in a liquidiser, together with the onions and garlic. Pass through a sieve and chill until needed. Just before serving, stir in the cream and adjust the seasoning.

Summer Carrot and Fresh Ginger Soup with Coriander Crème Fraîche

This is a wonderful summertime soup, topped with coriander crème fraîche to serve. It has a real freshness about it, which will leave you smiling.

1. In a large pan over a moderate heat, soften the onions in the oil without colouring. Add the carrots, mushrooms and ginger and allow to sweat over a low heat for 5 minutes, shaking the pan now and then.

2. Add the sherry and milk, cover with a lid and gently simmer until the carrots are soft.

3. Remove from the heat, blitz in a blender and pass through a sieve into a pan. Check the seasoning and whisk in a knob of butter. If the soup is too thick, thin it with a little milk or water.

SERVES 6

2 medium onions, sliced

25ml (1fl oz) olive oil

900g (2lb) English new season carrots, peeled and chopped

110g (4oz) button mushrooms, thinly sliced

75g (3oz) fresh root ginger, peeled and finely sliced

150ml (5fl oz) dry sherry

1 litre (1¾ pints) full-fat milk

knob of butter

seasoning

Coriander Crème Fraîche

1. Mix all the ingredients together and spoon a blob into the centre of each bowl of soup.

200ml (7fl oz) full-fat crème fraîche

1 large mild red chilli, finely chopped

1 small shallot, peeled and finely chopped

3 tbsp chopped fresh coriander

zest and juice of ½ lime

seasoning

Mousse of Petits Pois

SERVES 6

3 leaves of gelatine

275g (10oz) frozen or fresh petits pois

small bunch of fresh mint

pinch of sugar (optional)

75ml (3fl oz) double cream

seasoning

Served on its own on a hot day, this light, savoury, summery mousse is wonderful. But it's also really good with warm dishes such as scallops and crab – marrying hot and cold – with crisp fried bacon, or salad leaves with a light vinaigrette dressing and a croûton. Its alluring vibrant green colour makes it visually stunning: of course you eat first with your eyes and when things look this good, they invariably taste good too! I'd always go for petits pois as they have a distinctly sweeter flavour, but you can use frozen garden peas.

1. Place the gelatine leaves in a tray of cold water to soften.

2. Bring 200ml (7fl oz) water to the boil in a pan. Add the peas and the mint, bring back to the boil and cook for about 3 minutes. Remove from the heat.

3. Blitz immediately in a liquidiser, then while the purée is still hot, remove the gelatine leaves from the tray. Squeeze out any excess water, add to the purée and blitz again. Pass the purée through a sieve into a bowl, taste and season, adding a little sugar if you wish.

4. Set aside to cool completely. When the purée starts to set, whip the cream to soft peaks and fold it in. Cover with clingfilm and place in the fridge to allow the mousse to set completely.

Fillet of Beef Niçoise

This is a really good salad with a classic vinaigrette that can all be prepared well in advance – the vinaigrette will keep for several days in an airtight jar in the fridge. Using fillet of beef rather than tuna does play into the hands of the French, who refer to us as 'les rosbifs' but it also makes the dish more British. I like to serve the beef still warm but you can just as well serve it cold if you prefer.

1. Prepare all the salad ingredients well in advance and make the dressing: in a bowl, whisk together the vinegar, Dijon mustard, honey and garlic. Season with salt and pepper. Slowly add the oil, whisking continuously, taste and season then add the lemon juice and shallot.

2. To cook the beef; pre-heat the oven to 200°C/400°F/Gas mark 6.

3. Heat a frying pan large enough to take the whole fillet and, once very hot, add a good splash of olive oil. Place the fillet in the hot pan to seal, turning until browned all over.

4. Remove from the pan and place on a trivet in a roasting tin; season well. Roast in the pre-heated oven for 20–30 minutes, depending on how well cooked you want it to be: after 20 minutes it will be rare. Remove from the oven and rest for at least 10 minutes.

5. To assemble the salad, break the lettuce hearts into a large bowl or serving plate. Arrange all the remaining ingredients, apart from the parsley, on top. When ready to serve, season the salad and top with the beef, cut into thick slices. Scatter over the chopped parsley.

SERVES 6

1 fillet of beef, weighing about 1kg (2lb 4oz)
olive oil, for frying

For the salad:
4 Little Gem lettuce hearts
3 free-range eggs, hard boiled
12 small potatoes, scraped and boiled with a sprig of fresh mint until tender
a couple of handfuls of broad beans, blanched and skinned
18 small black olives
6 radishes, quartered
125g (4½oz) feta cheese, broken into chunks
3 slices of white bread, cubed, brushed with olive oil and baked until crisp
1 small can salted anchovy fillets, sliced lengthways
3 large vine tomatoes skinned and quartered
1 large red onion, peeled and sliced into rings
1 small jar artichoke hearts
1 bunch of flatleaf parsley, chopped

For the dressing:
2 tbsp red wine vinegar (or Raspberry Vinegar, page 107)
1 tsp Dijon mustard
1 tsp clear honey
1 large garlic clove, peeled and finely chopped
175ml (6fl oz) extra virgin olive oil
squeeze of lemon juice
1 small shallot, peeled and finely chopped
seasoning

Avocado Ice Cream

Like the Sweetcorn Ice Cream (page 56), this is another savoury ice cream that will no doubt intrigue you as to how good it can be! All I will say is that the proof of the pudding is in the eating: light and refreshing, it can be served on its own or as an accompaniment to crab, lobster or a summery tomato salad.

SERVES 6

75ml (3fl oz) milk

50g (2oz) caster sugar

3 large, fresh mint sprigs

2 really ripe avocados, peeled and stones removed

55ml (2fl oz) white wine

juice of 1 lemon

Maldon sea salt flakes

1. Place the milk, sugar, 75ml (3fl oz) water and mint in a pan. Bring to simmering point, then remove from the heat and set aside to infuse and cool.

2. Strain into a liquidiser, then add the avocados, white wine, lemon juice and a good pinch of salt. Blitz and pass through a fine sieve.

3. Churn in an ice cream maker, then freeze in a suitable container. If you don't have an ice cream maker, pour the mixture into a suitable container and place in the freezer. Take it out of the freezer about every 20 minutes and stir or whisk it until it is too thick to do so any more.

Spiced Duck Breast with Roast Pineapple

You need a good ripe pineapple for this. Slice the top and bottom off the pineapple, stand it on a chopping board and then using a sharp knife, peel the pineapple, trying to ensure you remove all the brown eyes. Buttery mashed potatoes and new season's carrots both go well with this dish.

1. Pre-heat the oven to 180°C/350°F/Gas mark 4.

2. Begin by cooking the pineapple: over a gentle heat, place the sugar in a shallow pan or frying pan with an ovenproof handle. The sugar will start to caramelise around the edge of the pan first, so it is important to keep giving the pan a good shake, not a stir.

3. When the sugar is an even light caramel all over, add the vinegar and allow to bubble a little. With the pan still on the heat, add 250ml (9fl oz) water, the star anise and cloves. Scrape the seeds from the vanilla pod and add these to the pan, together with the pod. Turn up the heat and allow to simmer for a minute or two.

4. Add the pineapple to the pan, turn the heat down a little and allow to bubble gently for 5 minutes, basting all the time with caramel as you do so.

5. Cover the pan with foil and place in the pre-heated oven for about 45 minutes, or until the pineapple has softened. Remove from the oven, place over a gentle heat and mix in the chilli, butter and lemon juice to taste. Check the seasoning.

6. Serve immediately with the duck or set aside to re-heat gently when needed.

7. To cook the duck: pre-heat the oven to 180°C/350°F/Gas mark 4.

8. Using a sharp knife score the skin of the duck breasts at about 1cm (½ inch) intervals, being careful not to pierce the flesh.

9. Heat a frying pan over a low heat, and place the duck breasts in the pan skin side down. Fry really gently for a good 5 minutes to colour the skin well. Season the flesh side and once the skin is well coloured, turn the breasts over and very quickly (literally seconds) seal the flesh side.

SERVES 6

150g (5oz) caster sugar

3 tbsp red wine vinegar

4 star anise

4 cloves

1 vanilla pod

1 medium-sized ripe pineapple, peeled but left whole

1 large chilli, seeded and finely chopped

25g (1oz) butter

juice of 1 lemon

6 Gressingham or Barbary duck breasts

seasoning

10. Remove the duck breasts from the pan and place on a trivet in a roasting tin. Roast in the pre-heated oven for 4–6 minutes (this will give you pink duck), then set aside in a warm place to rest for a couple of minutes.

11. Carefully reheat the pineapple, remove from the pan and slice thinly on to serving plates. Carve the duck breasts into slices and place on top of the pineapple. Serve immediately, spooning over a little of the juices the pineapple was cooked in.

Cod Ceviche

Because there is no cooking involved in this recipe its success depends on the fish being vibrantly fresh and of the highest quality – frozen cod would not be suitable. It is also important that you use a really sharp knife to cut the fish as it must be cleanly cut and not 'shredded'. Ceviche – a term used for marinating fish in citrus juices so the acidic citrus then 'cooks' the fish – may not be for the faint-hearted, but it is really delicious, especially on a warm summer's evening with a glass of lager and some fresh bread to mop up the juices. This works equally well with monkfish, sole, halibut, salmon or even scallops, as long as they are really fresh out of the water.

1. Cut the cod into thin strips and arrange them on a large flat plate. Sprinkle with flakes of sea salt and a good grinding of black pepper, then scatter over the chillies and red onion.

2. Pour the lime juice all over the fish, then cover with clingfilm and place in the fridge for at least 5 hours or, better still, overnight; the lime juice will 'cook' the fish and turn it opaque.

3. When you are ready to serve the ceviche, chop the coriander and mint. Sprinkle these over the fish, along with the lime zest.

SERVES 6

500g (1lb 2oz) cod fillet, skinned and boned
2 red chillies, finely chopped
1 medium red onion, peeled and thinly sliced
zest and juice of 4 limes
small bunch of fresh coriander
small bunch of fresh mint
Maldon sea salt flakes
freshly ground black pepper

CASUAL
SUP

OUTDOOR
PERS

From a laid-back supper in the back garden to a sizzling barbecue, summer food should be quick, simple and easy. No one wants to spend hours in the kitchen on a warm day when they could be outside! We don't entertain much at all, but if we do have friends round we aim to eat outside. My favourite meal would be half a lobster, shell-on prawns, crab and salad and some nice bread. It takes little work but relies on top-quality, fresh ingredients. Cooking should always be less about a prima donna chef and more about good ingredients.

I enjoy cooking at home – at work it's quite complex so at home I make simple dishes, mostly fish in the summer months when Tracy bans the Aga! Both the boys love sea bass; in fact, when staying with friends, Harry went into Wells fish and chip shop and asked if they did sea bass and chips! We cook plaice, mackerel and bass – I often tempura them, as in the recipe on page 155. I reckon any child would eat that, even those who say they don't like fish! Many of the recipes in the book are designed for family eating. Tracy cooks at home too and is a whiz with the Aga – I reckon they're only good for warming your bottom and for putting the ironing on, but she makes a fabulous crumble and chicken and mushroom pie.

One of my favourite activities in summer is to have a barbecue. Again, fish features heavily – it's great cooked on the barbecue as long as it's firm-fleshed, so monkfish, half a lobster or scallops are perfect. Asparagus also barbecues really well. There are a couple of recipes in the book that would also be great cooked on the barbecue – Norfolk-style New Potatoes with Bacon, Soya Beans and Samphire (see page 146) wrapped in foil and drizzled with rapeseed oil would be brilliant, as is Bouillabaisse in a Bag (page 152).

Refreshing summer drinks are also crucial. Pimm's doesn't really taste of alcohol so I much prefer a mojito. I was given one at Ronnie Scott's on a staff trip to London two years ago; its rum content gives it more appeal but it does need loads of mint, lime and sugar syrup – a great summer drink as it's so refreshing. I'd definitely drink mojitos with barbecue food.

Norfolk-style New Potatoes with Bacon, Samphire and Soya Beans

This is called Norfolk-style because my favourite potato variety, Juliette, is harvested locally, at the same time that the samphire comes up on the mud flats. Samphire is picked all along the north Norfolk coast and has become as synonymous with the county as Cromer crab. The samphire season more or less follows on from asparagus and it is treated in cooking in much the same way. As samphire is slightly salty, remember not to add salt to the cooking water and serve with unsalted butter. Soya beans are widely available frozen from supermarkets, but if you have trouble finding them, you could just as easily use young broad beans.

SERVES 6

225g (8oz) samphire

500g (1lb 2oz) medium new potatoes, scraped and quartered

2 shallots, finely chopped

2 garlic cloves, finely chopped

a little olive oil

175g (6oz) smoked English streaky bacon, chopped into lardons

125g (4½oz) soya beans, skins removed

large knob of unsalted butter

freshly ground black pepper

1. Begin by preparing the samphire: strip the fronds from the main stalks, wash thoroughly and then blanch by plunging into unsalted, boiling water for 30 seconds. Refresh in iced water, drain thoroughly and set aside.

2. Place the new potatoes in a large pan of salted water, bring to the boil and cook until just tender; drain thoroughly.

3. While the potatoes are cooking, heat a large frying pan and fry the shallots and garlic in a little olive oil. Add the lardons of bacon and cook well. Next, add the drained new potatoes to the bacon and, with the pan still on the heat, continue to cook, shaking the pan as you do so until the potatoes are coloured all over. Add the samphire and soya beans and, finally, a large knob of unsalted butter.

4. Season with pepper only, tossing thoroughly to make sure that everything is heated through. Serve immediately.

NORFOLK NEW POTATOES and SAMPHIRE

Eating outdoors demands rustic food and there's nothing earthier than potatoes and samphire, a true local speciality found on the salt marshes along the north Norfolk coast.

There's nothing like new potatoes – if I see someone selling some on a roadside stall I have to buy them! There's a stall near Sheringham run by a guy I used to play cricket with and I bought the whole lot off him once. They're brilliant just scraped and cooked with a bit of mint.

Samphire, a wild edible plant that grows on estuarine mudflats, is another seasonal delight that's become trendy in smart London restaurants, with a price tag to match. Here, you can buy a bag of it from a roadside stall for about £1! It's picked between June and August (after which time it becomes woody), which makes it almost obligatory with any summer dish. It goes brilliantly with fish – its almost seaweedy nature complementing the soft flakes of fish or the freshness of seafood. It was an acquired taste for me, though. As children when we were on holiday on the north Norfolk coast, we used to eat it raw, but it was really salty. It was only later that I came to appreciate its affinity with summer foods.

Grilled Sardines with Salsa Verde

Think of outdoor summer eating and grilled sardines may well come to mind. Because of their simplicity, they're always an essential element of alfresco dining. All you need are really fresh, grilled sardines drizzled with a little good-quality olive oil and lemon juice, then sprinkled with flakes of sea salt. Get your fishmonger to gut, clean and open them out (butterfly). Herrings, fresh out of the North Sea, would be a good alternative if sardines are unavailable. Served with a big bowl of summer salad, what could be better? The salsa verde makes a really tasty alternative: don't add the chopped parsley or lemon juice until just before serving, as otherwise it tends to discolour the mixture in a rather unappetising way. Salsa verde is best when eaten freshly made.

1. Make the salsa verde. Place the mint leaves, capers, anchovies, garlic and olives on a chopping board and chop to a paste-like consistency. Scrape into a bowl and mash in the breadcrumbs. Add the mustard, pine nuts and olive oil and mix well. Finally, just before serving, stir in the lemon juice and chopped parsley, then season to taste.

2. When you are ready to grill the sardines, pre-heat the grill to high.

3. Brush the sardines with olive oil, place on to a grill pan, season and squeeze over a little lemon juice. Grill for 3–4 minutes on each side, turning so that they are lightly charred all over.

4. To serve, spoon over some salsa verde or drizzle with a little olive oil and lemon juice. Sprinkle with more sea salt to taste if you think it needs it.

SERVES 6

For the salsa verde:

4 tbsp chopped mint leaves

3 tbsp capers, rinsed and drained

6 anchovy fillets, roughly chopped

1 garlic clove, roughly chopped

8 black olives, roughly chopped

2 slices stale white bread, crumbed

1 tsp Dijon mustard

2 tbsp pine nuts

120ml (4fl oz) good-quality olive oil

1½ tbsp lemon juice

20g (3/4oz) flat-leaf parsley leaves, chopped

seasoning

Allow 2 really fresh sardines per person, gutted, cleaned and butterflied

olive oil

fresh lemon juice

sea salt flakes

freshly ground black pepper

Roasted Asparagus with Parma Ham, Boiled Egg and Parmesan

The dry climate of Norfolk is ideally suited to growing asparagus, one of my absolute favourite summer ingredients. We get ours locally from Wiveton Hall in Blakeney (a great pick-your-own destination) and from a lady at Marsham. As the asparagus season is relatively short, I like to enjoy them to the full, especially roasted or barbecued as they retain their shape and full flavour. This dish makes a delicious start to an alfresco meal, although you could build up the quantities and serve it as a main course. The anchovy dressing can be made well in advance and stored in the fridge in an airtight jar. The Parma ham can be wrapped around the asparagus ahead of time. You don't have to use a ridged frying pan; it just gives a more interesting appearance.

SERVES 6

For the dressing
1 tbsp Dijon mustard
1 tbsp red wine vinegar
1/2 tsp clear honey
150ml (5fl oz) extra virgin olive oil
12 anchovy fillets, finely chopped
good squeeze of lemon juice
seasoning

24 large asparagus spears
24 thin strips Parma ham
a little olive oil, for brushing
6 free-range eggs
50g (2oz) coarsely grated fresh Parmesan
salad leaves, to serve

1. Begin by making the dressing: in a bowl, combine the mustard and red wine vinegar; season with salt and pepper. Whisk in the honey, followed slowly by the olive oil. Finally, add the anchovies and a good squeeze of lemon juice. Set aside.

2. Pre-heat the oven to 200°C/400°F/Gas mark 6.

3. Trim the woody ends from the asparagus and wrap a strip of Parma ham round each spear, leaving the tips free.

4. Place the eggs in a pan of cold water and, over a high heat, bring to the boil. When the water starts to boil, reduce to a simmer and boil for 4 minutes. Using a slotted spoon remove the eggs from the water and peel immediately.

5. Meanwhile, heat a ridged frying pan until very hot, brush each asparagus and Parma ham spear with a little olive oil and place in the heated pan. Fry them, turning regularly as you do so, until well-coloured all over. Remove from the frying pan and place on a baking sheet. Transfer to the oven and roast for 5 minutes.

6. To serve, lay the asparagus on to a warmed plate, place an egg next to them and cut in half. Sprinkle with Parmesan and spoon over some of the dressing. Serve with seasoned salad leaves, lightly dressed with the same dressing.

Bouillabaisse in a Bag!

In truth, this is a million miles away from the fish soup made in Marseilles. The similarities, though, are chunks of varied fishes and the fact that, when you bring this to the table, no one can fail to be transported to the sun-soaked Mediterranean when they open up the fragrant parcels. A meal in itself, this can be cooked in the oven as well as on the barbecue for about the same length of time.

1. Pre-heat the oven to 180°C/350°F/Gas mark 4.

2. For each of the six parcels, lay three pieces of foil, each 30 x 30cm (12 x 12 inches) on top of each other on your work surface. Then, into the centre of each piece, place 2 tiger prawns, a piece of monkfish, a scallop and a piece of salmon, together with 1 quartered tomato, 1 tablespoon each of broad beans and peas and a slice of lemon. Drizzle over a tablespoon of white wine and a good splash of olive oil, top with a sprig of dill and season well.

3. Seal the foil parcels by gathering up the sides to the middle and crimping the edges. Place them on a baking sheet and cook in the pre-heated oven for 5–8 minutes. Serve immediately by handing each guest a parcel to open at the table.

SERVES 6

12 tiger prawns, shelled

350g (12oz) monkfish tails, membrane removed and cut into 6 pieces, each 50g (2oz)

6 large king scallops, sliced through the middle horizontally

350g (12oz) salmon fillet, pinboned and cut into 6 pieces, each 50g (2oz)

6 tomatoes, cut into quarters

6 tbsp broad beans, skins removed

6 tbsp fresh or frozen petits pois

1 lemon, cut into 6 slices

6 tbsp white wine

olive oil

6 fresh dill sprigs

seasoning

Tempura of Prawns with Ginger-flavoured Mayonnaise

SERVES 6

For the mayonnaise:

1 egg
juice of 1 lime
2 tsp Dijon mustard or 1tsp English mustard powder
300ml (1/2 pint) sunflower oil
finely grated fresh root ginger (use a microplane grater)
extra lime juice (optional)
grated zest of 1/2 lime
seasoning

For the prawn tempura:
50g (2oz) cornflour
200g (7oz) self-raising flour
1 tsp baking powder
1/2 tsp salt
sparkling mineral water
vegetable oil, for frying.
18 large tiger prawns, shells removed

When you're eating outside, you need food that's easy to serve and eat – and this one definitely fits the bill as it's practically finger food. This is a great recipe to serve to children, even those who claim they don't like seafood! They all seem to love the tempura batter. The ginger simply gives a subtle element to a gorgeous accompaniment but you'll be surprised by how much you need to add. I like to buy tiger prawns and shell them myself so I can use the shells to make a soup. The dry ingredients can be combined and stored in an airtight container if you want to prepare them in advance.

1. Prepare the mayonnaise first: place the egg and 2 tablespoons lime juice in the bowl of a food processor, together with the mustard and a good seasoning of salt and pepper.

2. Whiz on a high speed; turn off the machine and, using a spatula, scrape down the sides and bottom of the bowl to make sure everything is properly incorporated. Turn the machine back on and very slowly drizzle in the sunflower oil (the mixture will emulsify and thicken). Next, add the finely grated fresh ginger to taste, more lime juice if you feel it needs it and the lime zest. Finally check the seasoning. Chill in the fridge until needed.

3. When you are ready to prepare the tempura, make a batter by combining the dry ingredients with enough sparkling mineral water to make a runny, lumpy batter.

4. Meanwhile, in a heavy-based pan, heat the vegetable oil, which should come no higher than one-third of the way up the side of the pan, to 160°C/315°F.

5. Using a fork or wooden skewer, dip a prawn dip into the batter mixture, then drop it into the heated oil. Fry for about 1 minute until just golden-brown then, using a slotted spoon, remove from the oil and drain on kitchen paper. Continue cooking several at a time until all the prawns are cooked.

6. When ready to serve, heat the oil to 180°C/350°F then quickly fry the prawns once again to crisp. Drain and serve immediately with ginger-flavoured mayonnaise.

Rib-eye Steak with Red Onion Relish and Barbecue Sauce

SERVES 6

For the red onion relish

olive oil

6 medium red onions, peeled, halved and sliced

6 tbsp red wine vinegar

3 heaped tbsp dark muscovado sugar

seasoning

For the barbecue sauce

1 tbsp clear honey

25g (1oz) dark muscovado sugar

1/2 small bird's eye chilli, split and seeded

25g (1oz) fresh root ginger, chopped

juice of 2 limes

100ml (3 1/2 fl oz) pineapple juice

100ml (3 1/2 fl oz) orange juice

1 tsp Dijon mustard

1 garlic clove, peeled and roughly chopped

100ml (3 1/2 fl oz) red wine vinegar

4 tbsp tomato purée

good pinch of ground cumin

good pinch ground turmeric

2 tbsp brown sauce

6 rib-eye steaks, each 225g (8oz)

50g (2oz) beef dripping (or olive oil)

I'm a big fan of this particular cut of beef as I feel it has a deeper flavour and better texture than the more glamorous sirloin or fillet. At Morston, beef comes to us after being hung for five weeks and we then hang it for a further two weeks to enhance the flavour and tenderise the meat. You should be able to get beef dripping from your butcher. The barbecue sauce is really spicy and tangy – a million miles from some of the smoky, shop-bought varieties. It works really well with most meats and, like the red onion relish, can be made in advance and kept in the fridge.

1. First, make the red onion relish and the barbecue sauce. For the relish, heat a large pan over a high heat, then add a good splash of olive oil. Add the onions, frying them until they start to colour and stick. Add the vinegar and sugar, turn the heat down and cook over a low heat for 15–20 minutes until the liquid has just about evaporated.

2. Add 100ml (3 1/2 fl oz) water and turn the heat up to simmer, cooking until all the liquid has been absorbed and you have a relish-like consistency. Season to taste, remove from the heat and set aside. This can be served warm or cold.

3. For the barbecue sauce, mix all the ingredients together in a bowl, transfer to a liquidiser and blitz really well. Transfer to a pan and bring to the boil. Reduce to a simmer for about 10 minutes until the sauce has thickened slightly.

4. To cook the steaks, pre-heat the oven to 200°C/400°F/Gas mark 6.

5. Heat a large frying pan until almost starting to smoke. Add half the dripping then three of the steaks, turning to seal all over and colour well, seasoning as you do so. Remove from the pan, place on a trivet in a roasting tin and brush with the some of the sauce. Repeat with the other three steaks.

6. Roast the steaks in the pre-heated oven for 5 minutes if you want them rare, brushing them from time to time with the barbecue sauce. Leave to rest in a warm place before serving with the red onion relish and a bowl of barbecue sauce.

Duck Breasts with a Honey, Ginger and Soy Sauce Glaze and Pak Choi

The duck I use at Morston for cooking has to be Gressingham, a breed of duck that tends to be quite small, which means that one breast per person is ideal. These duck breasts can be roasted in the oven or cooked on the barbecue skin side down, two at a time to avoid fat dripping into the barbecue and causing it to flare up! With barbecuing, there is no need to seal the breasts first in a frying pan – just make sure the barbecue is really hot and ready before placing the duck breasts on to it. Roast butternut squash or new potatoes would make a great accompaniment.

1. Blitz the glaze ingredients really well in a liquidiser, then pour into a bowl.

2. Pre-heat the oven to 200°C/400°F/Gas mark 6.

3. Using a sharp knife, score the skin of the duck breasts, season well and set aside. Heat a frying pan over a medium heat and add a splash of olive oil. When it is hot, place the duck breasts in the pan, skin side down, and press down firmly to seal. When they are really well coloured, season them, turn over and briefly seal the flesh side.

4. Brush the flesh side of each breast with the honey glaze. Place on a trivet in a roasting tin, skin side up, then liberally brush again with the glaze.

5. Roast in the pre-heated oven for 10 minutes, turning and basting (or brushing) as much as you can. (Alternatively, you could cut the duck breasts into strips, which would cook much more quickly).

6. Remove from the oven and set aside somewhere warm to rest for 3–4 minutes.

7. Heat a frying pan, add a splash of sesame or olive oil followed by the pak choi and a splash of water. Stir-fry for 2 minutes (the pak choi should retain some crunch). Season and add the sesame seeds.

8. To serve, arrange some pak choi in the centre of each plate, then carve the duck on top of it.

SERVES 6

For the honey, ginger and soy sauce glaze:
175g (6oz) clear honey
4 tsp chopped fresh root ginger
55ml (2fl oz) light soy sauce
1 tsp Chinese five spice powder
1 tsp mild curry powder
2 garlic cloves
2 tbsp sesame oil
seasoning

6 Barbary or Gressingham duck breasts, skin left on
olive oil, for frying

For the pak choi:
6 pak choi, roughly chopped
sesame or olive oil, for frying
2 tbsp sesame seeds

Wild Mushroom Pizza

I like the idea of foraging for wild mushrooms but this can be fraught with danger and, to my mind, is best left to people who know what they're doing! This pizza can be served on its own or with lightly dressed salad leaves and crisp fried bacon. Instead of using fresh yeast, you could use 1 tsp fast-action dried yeast. If so, mix it with the sugar, water and oil then add to the combined flour-and-salt mixture. This pizza could also be made by hand.

1. First, make the dough: place the flour and salt in the bowl of an electric food mixer and combine using the dough hook or 'K' beater attachment. In another bowl, combine the yeast and sugar using your fingertips. When the mixture become runny, add the sparkling water and olive oil.

2. Turn the electric mixer back on and slowly pour in the liquid, then leave the machine to knead the dough until smooth and elastic. Remove the bowl from the machine, cover with a clean damp tea towel and leave in a warm place to prove for about 40 minutes.

3. Meanwhile, prepare the toppings, seasoning the mushrooms and cream with salt and pepper.

4. Take the risen dough out of the bowl and, on a very lightly floured surface, knock it back. Next, roll the dough out into a rectangle about 30 x 25cm (12 x 10 inches). Place the dough on a non-stick baking sheet of similar proportions and refrigerate for about 30 minutes.

5. Pre-heat the oven to 200°C/400°F/Gas mark 6.

6. Remove the dough from the fridge and allow it to come up to room temperature (about 20 minutes). Brush the top with olive oil, prick with a fork to prevent bubbles from forming and bake in the pre-heated oven for about 10 minutes.

7. Remove from the oven, spread the onions over the top and then sprinkle over the mushrooms and tarragon. Using your thumb, make 12 indentations evenly over the top of the pizza and break a quail's egg into each one. Finally, pour the reduced cream all over the top and return to the oven for 5–10 minutes to ensure the quail's eggs are cooked.

SERVES 6

For the dough:

225g (8oz) strong plain flour

1 tsp salt

10g (1/2oz) fresh yeast

1/2 tsp caster sugar

120ml (4fl oz) sparkling water

2 tbsp olive oil, plus extra for brushing

For the toppings:

1 medium onion, peeled, sliced and sautéed in olive oil till soft

250g (9oz) mixed wild mushrooms, chopped and very briefly sautéed in a splash of olive oil

1 tbsp chopped fresh tarragon

12 quails' eggs

275ml (1/2 pint) double cream, reduced and thickened

seasoning

Bruschetta of Roasted Beetroot, Goats' Cheese, Balsamic and Rocket

These make wonderful casual outdoor supper food – rustic and not too smart is the way forward here. Use ciabatta bread or, if you can't get it, good-quality white bread with large croûtons cut from the centre of each slice. Good news for busy cooks is that the bruschette can be prepared in advance and warmed up to serve. A crumbly goats' cheese works well for this and, although there are many good British goats' cheeses, I suggest you use your own personal favourite.

SERVES 6

(2 bruschette per person)

55ml (2fl oz) good-quality olive oil, plus extra for drizzling

1 garlic clove, peeled and finely chopped

12 slices ciabatta bread, cut at an angle

black olive tapenade, for spreading

3 medium, cooked beetroot, peeled and thinly sliced

200g fairly crumbly goats' cheese

25g (1oz) toasted pine nuts, roughly chopped

60g (2½oz) pack wild rocket leaves

4 tbsp good-quality thick and syrupy aged balsamic vinegar

seasoning

1. Pre-heat the grill to high.

2. In a small bowl, mix together the olive oil and garlic, then liberally brush this on both sides of the bread. Place the bread on a rack under the grill and toast both sides.

3. Pre-heat the oven to 180°C/350°F/Gas mark 4.

4. Spread each slice of toasted ciabatta with tapenade, then add a thin slice of beetroot, seasoning as you do so. Top with crumbled goat's cheese, scatter over some chopped pine nuts and drizzle with a little more olive oil.

5. Place on a baking tray and put in the oven for a few minutes to warm through, allowing the goat's cheese to soften. Remove from the oven and serve with rocket leaves drizzled with a little balsamic vinegar.

Bobotie

I first discovered bobotie – a cross between shepherd's pie and moussaka – many years ago when cooking in Cape Town. Although a custard topping for lamb may seem unusual, it wouldn't appear odd in South Africa, where this traditional dish originates. Try it – it's really good. You can use minced lamb from the supermarket but as I have my own mincer I prefer to do it myself. You can make the base for the bobotie well in advance (and indeed even freeze it). Then, when you are ready to serve, all you need to do is make the topping and cook it. Start this the day before by soaking the sultanas in brandy overnight.

1. Heat a large pan, add the olive oil and fry the onions and garlic till soft and just coloured. Add the lamb and continue to fry briskly, stirring continuously, till coloured.

2. Stir in the tomato purée, curry powder and quince jelly, bring to a slow boil and simmer for about 20 minutes until cooked.

3. Taste and season with salt and pepper, adding a little more curry powder if liked. Stir in the soaked sultanas and almonds and transfer to a Pyrex dish approx 30 x 20 x 7.5cm (12 x 8 x 3 inches). Leave to cool.

4. Pre-heat the oven to 180°C/350°F/Gas mark 4.

5. Next make the custard topping: in a bowl, lightly whisk together the eggs, egg yolks, nutmeg and sugar. Stir in the whipping cream and brandy and season with salt and pepper.

6. Strain through a sieve into a jug, then carefully pour this mixture over the lamb.

7. Place the Pyrex dish in a roasting tin and pour in enough hot water to come halfway up the sides. Cook in the pre-heated oven for about 40 minutes, or until the custard is set and lightly coloured. Serve immediately.

SERVES 8

3 tbsp sultanas, soaked overnight in 2 tbsp brandy

25ml (1fl oz) olive oil

3 medium onions, peeled and chopped

2 garlic cloves, finely chopped or grated

1.5kg (3lb 5oz) lean lamb, preferably shoulder, finely minced

6 tbsp tomato purée

2 tbsp mild curry powder

3 tbsp quince jelly or apricot jam

3 tbsp chopped almonds, toasted

seasoning

For the custard topping

4 eggs, plus 2 egg yolks

a little grated fresh nutmeg

pinch of sugar

570ml (1 pint) whipping cream

splash of brandy

INGS

Like afternoon tea, puddings are a great tradition in this country, from the steamed puds of the winter months to light, creamy concoctions for summer eating. For me, fruit is the essential ingredient in a summery pudding. Seasonality is always important and from May to September there's an abundance of home-grown soft fruit, so don't go looking for fruit from abroad. It's all about raspberries, strawberries and blackcurrants.

Pudding is the most important element of a meal as it's the last thing people remember, so you need to finish on a high note. I see it as an opportunity to do something quite artistic – you can decorate it and make it look good. You have to have cream! It's not an everyday thing so a drizzle of double cream is essential – everything in moderation is fine.

I go for puddings rather than cheese every time, although we're producing much better cheeses in this country nowadays. Cheesecake is a great favourite with me too. The one in this chapter is so easy and doesn't need cooking. My old boss, John Tovey at Miller Howe, used to use gelatine in his cheesecakes in the 1980s but we don't need to do that now. There's very little that's new in cooking but things do change a bit.

Treacle tart has an association with Norfolk, as does Parson Woodforde's Charter Pudding, which appears in *The Diary of a Country Parson*. It's a bit like a crème brulée – another of my favourites which, in this book, has been infused with lemon balm, an echo of medieval herb-scented desserts.

Gooseberry Fool

Generally at their best in July, gooseberries usually need plenty of sugar but I quite often buy wonderful sweet, almost wine-like purple gooseberries from my supplier Desmond MacCarthy. They've been on the vine longer which gives a more intense flavour. To my knowledge, there are two ways of making fools: one is to just poach your fruit with sugar, blitz, fold in some whipped cream and serve. The other way – which I believe gives the best result – is to make a custard, add this to the fruit then fold in the cream. If you wish, you could serve this either in a large bowl or in individual glasses with a little gooseberry purée in the base. Serve with Almond Thins (see next page).

I. Begin by making the gooseberry purée: combine all the ingredients in a pan with 55ml (2fl oz) water and, over a moderate heat, bring to a gentle simmer. Cook until the gooseberries are very soft, then remove from the heat. Blitz in a liquidiser and pass through a fine sieve into a bowl; set aside to cool.

2. To make the custard, place half the cream in a heavy-based pan with the vanilla pod and seeds. Bring gently to a simmer, then remove from the heat and leave to infuse for a while.

3. In a bowl, whisk together the egg yolks and sugar. Bring the cream back to simmering point and, whisking all the time, pour it over the eggs and sugar. Return the mixture to the pan and stir continuously over a low heat until the custard just coats the back of a spoon. Remove from the heat, pass through a sieve into another bowl and allow to cool.

4. Mix the cooled purée and custard together in a bowl. Whip the remaining 275ml (10fl oz) double cream to soft peaks and fold into the mixture. Place the gooseberry fool in the fridge until needed.

SERVES 6 GENEROUSLY

For the gooseberry purée
250g (9oz) ripe gooseberries
75g (3oz) caster sugar
55ml (2fl oz) water
4 tbsp elderflower cordial, preferably Belvoir

For the custard:
550ml (20fl oz) double cream
1/2 vanilla pod, split, with seeds scraped out
4 egg yolks
50g (2oz) caster sugar

Almond Thins

50g (2oz) icing sugar
50g (2oz) very soft butter
50g (2oz) egg white
50g (2oz) plain flour
50g (2oz) ground almonds
pinch of ground ginger
2 tbsp flaked almonds

These wafer-thin biscuits go sublimely well with the Gooseberry Fool on the previous page, though are equally good eaten on their own at any time of the day. They can be made well in advance as long as you keep them in an airtight container. This makes quite a large amount of biscuit dough, but it keeps well in the fridge for up to a week, so could be used as needed.

1. Pre-heat the oven to 180°C/350°F/Gas mark 4.

2. In a bowl, cream the sugar and butter and beat well. Add the remaining ingredients, except for the flaked almonds, and beat together really well. Leave to rest in the fridge for at least 30 minutes.

3. Cover a baking sheet with good-quality silicone-coated greaseproof paper. Using a palette knife, spread the mixture very thinly on to the greaseproof paper to make biscuits about 7.5cm (3 inches) x 2.5cm (1 inch).

4. Scatter over the flaked almonds and bake in the pre-heated oven for about 10 minutes until the biscuits are golden-brown.

5. Remove from the oven and, while still hot, use a palette knife to ease the biscuits carefully off the greaseproof paper and on to a wire rack to cool. Store in an airtight container.

Fresh Cherry Clafoutis with Kirsch and White Chocolate

SERVES 6

310g (11oz) large pitted black cherries

4 tbsp Kirsch or rum

40g (1½oz) plain flour

50g (2oz) ground almonds

50g (2oz) caster sugar

3 eggs, beaten

4 tbsp melted butter, plus extra for buttering ramekins

275ml (10fl oz) double cream, plus extra for serving

6 x 2.5cm (1 inch) squares white chocolate

icing sugar, for dusting

Clafoutis is a classic French cherry-and-batter pudding from the Limousin region of France. Lovely served warm, it can be prepared in the morning then baked when required. I've used black cherries because they're the traditional choice for a clafoutis, but most soft fruits could be used – I've also had brilliant results with raspberries and blackcurrants. If fresh cherries are difficult to find, you could use tinned ones or, for a special occasion, the small bottled griottine cherries.

1. Place the cherries and Kirsch in a bowl and leave to marinate for at least 1 hour.

2. Meanwhile, prepare the batter: place the flour, ground almonds, caster sugar, eggs, melted butter and double cream into a food processor. Blitz well, then pass through a sieve into a jug and leave to settle.

3. Pre-heat the oven to 180°C/350°F/Gas mark 4.

4. Place 6 large, well-buttered ramekins on to a baking sheet. Divide the cherries and white chocolate among the ramekins. Pour the marinating juice from the cherries into the batter, mix well and pour this over the cherries and chocolate to just fill the ramekins.

5. Bake in the pre-heated oven for about 35–40 minutes until you have a light-brown, sponge-like topping. Remove the clafoutis from the oven, dust with icing sugar and serve with the whipped double cream.

Vanilla and Ginger Cheesecake with Poached Rhubarb

Every year I seem to come up with a new cheesecake recipe and have gone from a baked one to one set with gelatine and now this one, my current favourite. I love the crunchy base provided by the Ginger Nuts. This cheesecake is best served at room temperature. If rhubarb is unavailable, use any summer fruit lightly poached in sugar (stock) syrup; strawberries or blueberries work particularly well.

1. Line the base and the sides of a 20cm (8 inch) high-sided cake tin with a removable base with good-quality greaseproof paper.

2. Pre-heat the oven to 150°C/300°F/Gas mark 2.

3. To make the cheesecake: blitz the ginger biscuits with the melted butter in a food processor. Press the biscuit base evenly and firmly over the base of the lined cake tin. Place in the centre of the pre-heated oven and bake for 10 minutes. Remove from the oven (but keep the oven on for the rhubarb) and allow to cool.

4. Meanwhile, make the poached rhubarb: place the rhubarb on a baking tray, then sprinkle over the sugar and the orange zest and juice. Cover with clingfilm, place in the pre-heated oven and bake for about 25 minutes until the rhubarb is completely cooked but has still retained its shape. Allow to cool.

5. Then, in a bowl, using a wooden spoon, beat together really well the cream cheese, crème fraîche, mascarpone cheese, caster sugar, vanilla extract and lime zest and juice, making sure the mixture is as smooth as possible.

6. In another bowl, whisk the cream to stiff peaks and fold this into the cream cheese mixture, making sure that everything is well incorporated. Spread the mixture over the biscuit base, smooth over the top then place into the fridge for 1 hour or overnight to firm up.

7. When ready to serve, remove the cheesecake from the cake tin and place on to a plate or board. Serve the cheesecake, cut into slices, with the cooled poached rhubarb.

SERVES 6 GENEROUSLY

For the cheesecake
12 Ginger Nut biscuits
50g (2oz) unsalted butter, melted
175g (6oz) full-fat cream cheese (such as Philadelphia)
75g (3oz) crème fraîche
125g (4½oz) mascarpone cheese
125g (4½oz) caster sugar
1 tsp vanilla extract
finely grated zest of 1 lime, plus the juice of ½ lime
275ml (10fl oz) double cream

For the poached rhubarb
6 sticks forced rhubarb, cut into even-sized batons
150g (5oz) light muscovado sugar
zest and juice of 1 orange

Roasted Almond Ice Cream

225g (8oz) flaked almonds
275ml (10fl oz) full-fat milk
275ml (10fl oz) double cream
1/2 tsp vanilla extract
75g (3oz) caster sugar
6 egg yolks

I'm a bit of an ice cream buff and this one is my current favourite. It's unusual to get such a good, delicate toasted almond flavour in a pudding and that's what makes it worthwhile. Make sure you toast the almonds to a good colour to achieve the best flavour, but watch them really carefully or you'll burn them and be doing it 2 or 3 times – I've been there and done that! This goes really well with poached peaches, nectarines or plums, and will keep well in the freezer. Almonds also have a natural affinity with cherries, so this would be a wonderful accompaniment for Fresh Cherry Clafoutis with Kirsch and White Chocolate (see page 173).

1. Pre-heat the oven to180°C/350°F/Gas mark 4.

2. Place the almonds on a baking sheet and bake in the pre-heated oven for about 8–10 minutes, until they have roasted to a good golden colour (but keep checking on them as they will suddenly turn and burn). Remove from the oven immediately.

3. Place the milk, cream and vanilla extract in a heavy-based pan and bring to a simmer. Remove from the heat, add the roasted almonds, cover tightly with clingfilm and leave to infuse for 30 minutes.

4. In a bowl, whisk together the sugar and egg yolks until pale and creamy. Bring the infused milk and cream back to simmering point then quickly strain the mixture into a jug to remove the almonds. Pour the hot milk and cream over the eggs and sugar, whisking continuously.

5. Return the custard mixture to the pan and over a low heat and without boiling, stir continuously with a wooden spoon until the custard is thick enough to coat the back of the spoon. Remove from the heat immediately, pass through a fine sieve into a bowl and leave to cool completely.

6. Churn in an ice-cream machine then freeze in a suitable container.

Plum Ripple Ice Cream

SERVES 6

275g (10oz) Victoria plums, damsons or any other variety of plum

50g (2oz) light muscovado sugar

570ml (1 pint) whipping cream

1 vanilla pod, split

6 egg yolks

110g (4oz) caster sugar

We have a walled garden in Morston with a Victoria plum tree in the corner. One year, after a massive crop of plums, we decided to experiment with them: it's only so often you can serve poached plums. One day I decided to make plum ripple ice cream. What a result! Any variety of plum – or, if you can get them, damsons or early river plums – would work equally well, as would raspberries, strawberries or blackcurrants.

1. Halve the plums, remove the stones and place in a pan, then sprinkle over the brown sugar and add 4 tablespoons water. Cook the plums over a gentle heat until very soft, then blitz in a liquidiser and leave to cool.

2. Place the cream in a pan, then scrape the vanilla seeds in, followed by the pod. Bring slowly up to the boil, remove from the heat and set aside to infuse for 30 minutes. Remove the vanilla pod.

3. Meanwhile, in a bowl combine the egg yolks and caster sugar and whisk until smooth and pale. Bring the cream just back to a simmer and add to the egg yolks and sugar, while continuing to whisk. Return to the pan.

4. Place the pan over a low heat and, stirring continuously with a wooden spoon, cook the custard until it coats the back of the spoon. Take off the heat, pass through a fine sieve into a bowl and allow to cool completely.

5. Churn the custard in an ice-cream machine. When it is nearly frozen, scoop some of the mixture into a suitable container. Spread over some of the plum purée, then repeat with another layer or two before placing the container in the freezer.

My Favourite Summer Trifle

I'm a great fan of sticky, sweet, gooey nursery puddings and can never resist homemade trifle, with a floppy layer of cream on top. I don't see why trifle has to be associated just with Christmas – why not enjoy a good trifle in summertime using fresh poached summer fruits as I've done here? As with any trifle, it's not worth making a small one: this version serves 10, so you will need a 2.6-litre (4-pint) bowl. You can prepare the various components well in advance, then assemble them before placing in the fridge.

1. Pre-heat the oven to 180°C/350°F/Gas mark 4.

2. In a bowl, cream together the butter and sugar till pale and creamy (an electric whisk is good for this), then gradually add the eggs, a little at a time. Using a metal spoon or spatula, fold in the flour and add the orange zest and juice.

3. Pour the sponge mixture into a 20cm (8 inch) round cake tin, greased and lined with silicone baking parchment. Bake in the oven for about 30 minutes until springy to the touch. Remove from the oven, allow to rest for a couple of minutes then turn out onto a wire rack to cool.

For the jelly

1. Place the raspberries, sugar, white wine and 75ml (3fl oz) water in a pan. Bring slowly to the boil then turn down the heat and simmer for a few minutes. Meanwhile, place the gelatine leaves into a tray of cold water for a few minutes to soften.

2. Remove the raspberries from the heat and pass the mixture through a piece of muslin or a fine sieve over a jug to retain the juice. Take the softened gelatine from the tray, squeezing out any excess water as you do so, and stir into the still warm raspberry juice to dissolve. Allow to cool and set.

For the poached strawberries and raspberries

1. Place the water, sugar and lime juice in a pan and, over a moderate heat, bring to the boil. Remove from the heat, stir in the vanilla bean paste then add the fruits. Leave to steep until the fruits have 'fallen' but are not yet mushy.

SERVES 10

For the sponge
125g (4½oz) softened butter
125g (4½oz) caster sugar
3 eggs, beaten
125g (4½oz) self-raising flour
zest and juice of ½ orange

250g (9oz) raspberries
50g (2oz) caster sugar
75ml (3fl oz) white wine
3 gelatine leaves

120ml (4fl oz) water
75g (3oz) caster sugar
juice of 1 lime
½ tsp vanilla bean paste or extract
450g (1lb) strawberries, hulled
450g (1lb) raspberries

For the custard

1. Place the cream and milk in a pan together with the seeds scraped from the vanilla pod and the pod itself. Bring to the boil over a moderate heat.

2. In a bowl, whisk together the egg yolks, sugar and cornflour until light and creamy (an electric hand whisk is good for this). Once the cream has come to the boil, remove from the heat and immediately pour it over the eggs. Whisk well and return the custard to the pan over a moderate heat, stirring continuously with a wooden spoon until it coats the back of the spoon. Take off the heat, strain through a fine sieve and allow to cool and thicken.

275ml (10fl oz) double cream
150ml (5fl oz) full-fat milk
½ vanilla pod, split lengthways
4 medium egg yolks
75g (3oz) caster sugar
1 tbsp cornflour

Sugared Nuts

1. Place all the ingredients in a heavy-based, non-stick frying pan and, over a gentle heat, allow the nuts to caramelise (as soon as this starts to happen, stir the nuts occasionally). When they're a light, golden-caramel colour, remove them from the heat and turn out on to a piece of very lightly oiled greaseproof paper. Leave to cool.

25g (1oz) whole peeled hazelnuts
25g (1oz) pecan nuts, roughly chopped
25g (1oz) flaked almonds
110g (4oz) icing sugar
4 tbsp Grand Marnier

To assemble the trifle

1. Slice the sponge into three thin layers and place one layer in the base of a large glass bowl. Douse the sponge with about one-third of the sherry (6 tablespoons): this is only a guideline; if you wish to use more, it is up to you. Spread one-third of the poached fruits on top of the sherry-soaked sponge.

2. Break the jelly up with a fork and spread one-third of it over the fruits.

3. Repeat this process with two more layers of sponge, adding one-third of the sherry, fruit and jelly each time. Pour the thickened custard over the last layer of jelly.

4. Lightly whip the cream to the soft peak stage, then spread it over the custard. Place in the fridge to firm up. When ready to serve, break up the sugared nuts and scatter over the top.

275ml (10fl oz) dry sherry
275ml (10 fl oz) double cream

Blackcurrant Blitz: a Summery Fool and Sorbet

For the blackcurrant fool:
450g (1lb) blackcurrants
75g (3oz) caster sugar
275ml (10fl oz) whipping cream
1 vanilla pod, split
3 egg yolks
3 tbsp caster sugar
1 tbsp cornflour
275ml (10fl oz) double cream

For the blackcurrant sorbet:
450g (1lb) fresh or frozen blackcurrants
175g (6oz) caster sugar
juice of 1/2 lemon

Blackcurrants probably make the best fool, ice cream and soufflé, the reason being that those little black berries have a very intense flavour ... and this wonderful pudding is no exception. Serve it either in a large bowl or in individual glasses.

1. Place the blackcurrants in a pan with 75g (3oz) caster sugar and 4 tablespoons water. Bring to the boil and simmer slowly until very soft. Blitz in a liquidiser, pass through a sieve into a bowl and set aside to cool.

2. Meanwhile, pour the whipping cream into a heavy-based pan, and then scrape in the vanilla seeds and the empty vanilla pod. Bring slowly to the boil, then set aside for 30 minutes to infuse. Remove the vanilla pod.

3. Whisk the egg yolks, 3 tbsp sugar and cornflour together in a large bowl. Gently reheat the infused cream and, as soon as it reaches boiling point, pour it on to the egg yolk mixture, whisking all the time.

4. Return the custard to the pan and, over a low heat, stir continuously until it has thickened enough to coat the back of a spoon.

5. Immediately remove the pan from the heat, then pass the custard through a fine sieve into a bowl and allow to cool. When the custard is cold, pour in the blackcurrant purée and mix thoroughly.

6. Whisk the double cream to very soft peaks then fold this into the blackcurrant custard. Carefully pour into a glass dish and place in the fridge to firm.

For the blackcurrant sorbet

1. Place the blackcurrants, sugar and 150ml water into a pan. Over a moderate heat, bring to the boil and lightly cook the blackcurrants until very soft.

2. Blitz in a liquidiser, pass through a fine sieve into a jug and allow to cool completely. Stir in the lemon juice then churn in an ice cream machine. Store in the freezer in a suitable container.

SOFT SUMMER FRUIT

Soft fruits loom large in many of my teatime and pudding recipes as they're some of this country's best ingredients – and in Norfolk we're lucky to enjoy wonderful summer berries of all types.

Getting on well with our suppliers is crucial and we always listen to what they advise us is best at any one time. We get quite a bit of our soft fruit, as well as globe artichokes, from Wiveton Hall, near Blakeney, an impressive seventeenth-century manor house with a huge market garden and fruit fields that run down to the salt marshes – an idyllic spot where you can pick your own produce, buy local fruit, veg and meat and enjoy a seasonal lunch in the summer months. Local restaurateur Alison Yetman cooks simple seasonal food in the farm café there during the summer months and serves it in a wooden building painted in ice-cream colours of pink, pistachio and baby blue.

Wiveton Hall produces wonderful strawberries, raspberries and gooseberries that are second to none, the best I've ever eaten. We also get our blackcurrants (the inspiration behind Blackcurrant Blitz, page 183) and a host of other foods there. The owner, Desmond MacCarthy, is a real character. I once asked him for gooseberries and he laughingly informed me that I knew nothing about seasonality as they'd finished about a month before. And this to a chef who's built his whole reputation on working with seasonal food! When you buy food from local suppliers you have to like the people you're dealing with – and he's really got it right in terms of producing superb crops.

Strawberries come from Sharrington – one of the varieties they grow is Honeoye and they are the finest I have ever tasted. We make all our own jams and other preserves at Morston (see page 197 to buy by mail order) so good soft fruit is really important. Because it comes, literally, from just down the road, it keeps its just-picked freshness and also doesn't suffer from being transported across the country.

Pink Fizz Summer Fruit Jelly

Don't use your best vintage pink champagne for this – instead, choose a good sparkling rosé. I use an English rosé from Chilford Hall vineyards in Cambridgeshire. This jelly not only looks stunning but has a light, refreshing taste, and the reason I like to use fizz is that it gives a great sherbety tingle on the tongue!

1. Place the gelatine leaves in a tray of cold water for a few minutes to soften.

2. Next, place the sugar, the rosé wine and 150ml (5fl oz) of the pink sparkling wine in a pan and, over a low heat, allow the sugar to melt. Remove the softened gelatine from the water, squeezing out any excess water with your hands as you do so. Add the gelatine to the warmed sugar and wine mixture, stirring thoroughly to dissolve, then set aside to cool.

3. When the mixture is cool but has not yet set, very slowly (so you retain as much fizz as possible), stir in the remaining sparkling wine.

4. Add half the mixed fruit to a 900g (2lb) loaf tin (or terrine). Next, slowly pour in enough wine jelly mixture barely to cover the fruit, then place in the fridge (keep the remaining wine jelly mixture at room temperature as you don't want it to set at this stage).

5. When the jelly mixture in the fridge has just started to firm up, scatter the mint leaves over, if using, then fill the loaf tin with the rest of the fruit and cover with remaining wine jelly mixture. Cover tightly with clingfilm and leave overnight in the fridge to set.

6. When you are ready to serve, remove the loaf tin from the fridge, dip it very briefly into a bowl of hot water then turn the jelly out on to a plate. Slice with a serrated knife and serve with homemade ice cream.

SERVES 8

8 gelatine leaves
250g (9oz) caster sugar
150ml (5fl oz) rosé wine
75cl bottle pink sparkling wine
125g (4 1/2 oz) raspberries
125g (4 1/2 oz) strawberries, quartered if large
125g (4 1/2 oz) blueberries
a few tiny mint leaves, or large chopped mint leaves (optional)

Peach Tarte Tatin

A classic French tarte tatin is an upside down apple tart in which you caramelise the apples in a pan with the pastry placed on top. I am changing this by using peaches because of the proliferation of peaches in the summer and because they marry really well with the butterscotch flavours of the caramel. You could also use nectarines if you wish.

SERVES 6-8

350g (12oz) good-quality butter puff pastry

150g (5oz) unsalted butter, softened

175g (6oz) light muscovado sugar

8 ripe peaches

Leaves from 1 fresh thyme sprig

Roasted Almond Ice Cream, to serve (see page 175)

1 x 23cm (9 inch) diameter deep-sided non-stick frying pan with a metal handle that can go into the oven.

1. Roll out the puff pastry into a circle a good 2.5cm (1 inch) larger in diameter than the frying pan you are using (I use a large dinner plate as a template).

2. Prick the pastry all over with a fork and place in the fridge to rest until needed.

3. Pat the butter all over the base of the frying pan and cover with the sugar. Place the pan over a moderate heat to melt the butter and dissolve the sugar. Turn up the heat a little until the butter and sugar has reached a light caramel stage, watching the pan all the time (this may sound difficult because you are already using brown sugar, but I would just take it to a slightly darker colour). Remove from the heat.

4. Halve the peaches and remove the stones (peel the peaches if you like but this is optional). Lay them, rounded side down, on top of the caramel and pack in tightly. Scatter the thyme leaves over the fruit, then cover with the pastry, tucking in any overlapping pieces. Place in the fridge while you pre-heat the oven to 200°C/400°F/Gas mark 6.

5. Place the pan in the pre-heated oven and cook for about 35 minutes until the pastry is golden. Remove from the oven and rest for 2 minutes before tilting the frying pan and spooning out any excess juices into a small pan. Over a moderate heat, reduce the liquid by half.

6. To serve, carefully turn the tarte tatin over on to a large serving plate. Serve with Roasted Almond Ice Cream or a good dollop of cream and some of the reduced peach juices spooned over.

Herb-infused Crème Brûlée with Raspberry Sorbet

Although it was popular to use herbs in sweet dishes in medieval cooking in this country, I have been generally against using herbs in crème brûlée because a good crème brûlée is perfect as it is, with that vanilla flavour and slight wobble. But one of our young commis chefs mistook lemon balm for mint and that's how this came about! If you can't find it, you could use fresh mint instead – or leave it as a plain brûlée! The raspberry sorbet makes enough for 6–8 so you can always leave some in the freezer for another time – obviously you need to make the sorbet in advance to give it enough time to freeze.

SERVES 6

1/2 vanilla pod

425ml (15fl oz) double cream

good handful of lemon balm

6 egg yolks

75g (3oz) caster sugar, plus 6 tsp
caster sugar to glaze

1. Pre-heat the oven to 140°C/275°F/Gas mark 1.

2. Using a sharp knife, halve the vanilla pod lengthways and scrape the seeds out into a pan. Add the vanilla pod, double cream and lemon balm and bring gently to the boil over a medium heat. Remove from the heat and set aside to infuse for at least 10 minutes.

3. Whisk the egg yolks and sugar in a bowl. Bring the cream nearly back to boiling and, while still whisking the egg and sugar mixture, pour the hot cream into it Pass the mixture through a fine sieve into a jug, then fill 6 ramekins, each 7.5cm (3 inches) in diameter.

4. Place the ramekins in a deep-sided roasting tin and pour in enough boiling water to come about one-third of the way up the sides of the ramekins. Place in the pre-heated oven and cook for about 50 minutes until the brûlées are just set, but still slightly wobbly in the centre when shaken gently. Remove from the oven, take the brûlées out of the tin and allow to cool before chilling in the fridge.

5. To serve, scatter 1 teaspoon of caster sugar over the top of each brûlée and glaze with a blowtorch until the surface turns a golden caramel colour.

Raspberry Sorbet

SERVES 6-8

450g (1lb) raspberries

150ml (1/4 pint) sugar (stock)
syrup (see pages 75 for recipe)

juice of 1/2 lemon, sieved

1. Blitz the raspberries in a food processor or blender, then press through a fine sieve into a jug.

2. Stir in the sugar syrup, tasting as you do so (you may not need to use all of it; the idea is to have a mixture which is sweet and yet bursting with the flavour). Finally, stir in the lemon juice before churning in an ice cream machine.

Whim Wham (Boozy Cream with Peaches and Almonds)

SERVES 6

1 pack sponge fingers (you need about 24)

juice of 2 oranges, plus the zest of 1 orange

120ml (4fl oz) Grand Marnier or brandy

6 ripe peaches

425ml (15fl oz) double cream

Sugared Nuts, to serve (see recipe, page 180)

We're going back some years, but this used to be one of my mother's very favourite dinner-party puddings – her take on a dessert that dates back to the eighteenth century. I have adapted the recipe a bit and it is really easy to make. As with most things that taste wonderful, however, it is not necessarily good for the figure but as a child I loved the booziness of it, as well as the sponge fingers and lots of whipped cream! Where my mother got the recipe from I don't know, but I do know it tastes bloody good.

1. Break the sponge fingers into the base of a large, decorative glass bowl.

2. Mix the orange juice, zest and liqueur in a jug. Pour it over the sponge fingers and leave to soak for several hours, or even overnight.

3. Peel the peaches and cut them into fairly thick slices. Spread these over the liqueur-soaked sponge fingers. Whip the cream to soft peaks and spread this over the peaches. Cover with clingfilm and place in the fridge.

4. When ready to serve, spread the sugared nuts over the cream.

MY LITTLE BLACK BOOK

EATING OUT: LOCAL FAVOURITES

Café Wiveton Farm Café
Wiveton Hall, Holt, Norfolk NR25 7TE
www.wivetonhall.co.uk

Paul Whittome at The Hoste Arms
The Green, Burnham Market, King's Lynn, Norfolk PE31 8HD
01328 738777
www.hostearms.co.uk

Yellows
Norwich City, Carrow Road, Norwich, NR1 1JE
01603 218209
www.deliascanarycatering.com
An American-style diner and a great place to eat when out
with the children.

Cookies Crab Shop
The Green, Salthouse, Holt, Norfolk NR25 7AJ
01263 740352
www.cookies.shopkeepers.co.uk
Basic shack with cheap seafood platters, crab sandwiches
etc. Bring your own wine (and wine glasses)! Booking
essential or phone if you want the lobster platter and to
make sure they're open.

Bure Rive Cottage Restaurant
27 Lower Street, Horning, Norfolk NR12 8AA
01692 631421

SHOPS … AND OUR FAVOURITE SUPPLIERS FOR MORSTON HALL

The Cheese Society
1 St Martins Lane, Lincoln LN2 1HY
01522 511003
www.thecheesesociety.co.uk
Mainly English and French cheeses.

Deli Bakers & Larners
8-10 Market Place, Holt, Norfolk, NR25 6BW
01263 712244
www.bakersandlarners.com

The North Norfolk Fish Company
8 Stable Yard, Holt, NR25 6BN
01263 711913
www.northnorfolkfish.co.uk

Arthur Howell (butcher)
53 Staithe Street, Wells-next-the-Sea, Norfolk NR23 1AN
01328 710214

P&S (game dealer)
8 Bull Street, Holt NR25 6HP
01263 713227

Hastings vegetable supplier
41 The High Street, Sherringham, Norfolk NR26 8DS
01263 822878

Sharrington Strawberry Farm
Langham Road, Field Dalling NR25 7LG
01328 830311

Letheringsett Water Mill
River Side Road, Letheringsett, NR25 7YD
01263 713153
www.letheringsettwatermill.co.uk

Willie Weston (fish)
27 Queens Close, Blakeney, Holt NR25 7PQ
01263 741112
www.westonsofblakeney.co.uk

Ferrers Le Mesurier (wine merchant)
The Dower House, Parish Road, Stratton Strawless NR10 5LP
01603 279975

Premium Wine
8 Alston Road, Drayton High Road, Norwich NR6 5DS
01603 427554

Pointens Bros (milk)
Grange Farm, Stody, Melton Constable NR24 2EB

Hill Farm Oils
Cart Lodge Office, Hill Farm, Heveningham, Halesworth, Suffolk IP19 0ED
01986 798660
www.hillfarmoils.com

Preserves
www.morstonhall.com

Acknowledgements

Thank you to everyone who has supported me during the
writing of this book and in particular to a few people very
close to me, none more so than my wife Tracy and the
boys Harry and Sam. A special word of thanks to my father,
Bill, whose enthusiasm for home cooking seems as strong
now as it was years ago and a big thank you to my in-laws
Sid and Jan who come to the rescue to help look after the
boys whenever schedules don't quite work out as planned.

Thanks also to Neil Alston who manages to put down on
paper exactly what I am trying to say (and then shreds it!!)
and keeps a reality check on me when I get too 'cheffy'
and don't communicate with the home cook for whom
these recipes are written.

I am very proud of this book, it has captured everything I
hoped it would and encapsulates my beautiful North
Norfolk Coast. I have to say that Tara Fisher, the
photographer, and I seem to see the countryside through
the same lens. Thank you Tara for your wonderful work.

I would also like to thank the whole team at Morston Hall
and in particular Sam Wegg and Richard Bainbridge in the
kitchen and Liz in the office.

Thanks to Jo Hill the copyeditor for her tireless editing and
to all those who tested these recipes for me. Finally last,
but not least , to all the team at Virgin books, especially
Carolyn , Gareth and the Marketing and Publicity teams
who have been such a pleasure to work with.

Galton Blackiston
May 2009

Index